STRONG GIRLS

You ARE GOD's MASTERPIECE

(EPH. 2:10)

Developing Girls with Unstoppable Character, Confidence, and Courage

Jimmy Page   Grace Page

STRONG GIRLS

Developing Girls with Unstoppable *Character, Confidence, and Courage*

Jimmy Page   Grace Page

Unstoppable Warriors 37 LLC
6314 Spring Seed Way
Fort Collins, CO, 80528 USA

info@beastronggirl.com

Strong Girls: Developing Girls with Unstoppable Character, Confidence, and Courage

9798328683920 (paperback)

Cover and interior design by Franklin Lugenbeel.

ENDORSEMENTS

We need strong girls who grow into fearless women now more than ever. This book uses truth from the Bible to forge girls with grit, faith, and purpose; girls who stand up for what's right and change the world.

> **Riley Gaines**, author, speaker, 12x All-American swimmer, 2x Olympic Trial Qualifier, 5x SEC Champion, fearless advocate for women's rights, and host of Outkick's *"Gaines for Girls"* podcast

There is nothing more inspiring than seeing young women living out their purpose with character, confidence, and courage. Jimmy and his daughter Grace share the life-changing truths from their journey, and provide the tools to develop strong girls who become amazing women.

> **Kathryn Gordon**, wife, mom, businesswoman, bestselling author of *Relationship Grit,* and host of the *Kathryn for REAL!* podcast
> **Jon Gordon**, 17X bestselling author of *The One Truth, Energy Bus,* and *One Word*

The ideas and forces in our culture today can negatively impact a girl's self-image and confidence. Jimmy and Grace Page have developed a powerful three-step process to help girls overcome these negative influences and embrace God's perfect design for their lives. Sure, it's easier to ignore God's call than pursue it, but if you're like me, you'll read this book to have the courage to fulfill it!

> **Jacqueline Genova**, Founder of WellnStrong™, certified holistic nutritionist, wellness writer, and podcaster

As an Olympic Gold Medalist, having godly character, confidence and courage were a crucial part of my journey. In Strong Girls, Grace shares relatable stories and offers applicable advice to change your thoughts to work for you and not against you. This book is a must read for girls of all ages who want to live a life of hope and victory.

> **Leah Amico**, 3-Time Olympic Gold Medalist, Author, Speaker

What a wonderful gift father and daughter Jimmy and Grace Page have created for families. Through the experiences Grace lived growing up through transitions, and the power and grace that Faith in the supernatural transformation make available to us all, they share with us the truth of Godly principles, and practical applications to build them into readers' lives. This is especially given for daughters and fathers. Jimmy and Grace show The Way of Christ directly in real family life!

John Harbaugh, Head Coach of the Baltimore Ravens, Super Bowl XLVII Champion, 2019 NFL Coach of the Year, and #GirlDad

Strong Girls is a must read for every girl and young woman who dreams big dreams and strives to accomplish great things. This book helps you build an unshakeable foundation, empowering you to fearlessly create a future you can be proud of.

Marshi Smith, Co-Founder of ICONS – Independent Council on Women's Sports, NCAA & PAC-10 Swim Champion, 15x All-American, World Cup Medalist, and fearless warrior to save women's sports

Strong Girls is a faith-filled, encouraging read for girls and women of all ages. This book is so much more than something you read cover to cover and put on the bookshelf—there are simple and powerful tools to come back to again and again for strength and support. God perfectly designed girls with beauty, brains, brawn, and brilliance. What a gift this book will be for our daughters and so many girls around the world!

Julie W. Nee and **Amy P. Kelly**, co-authors of *You Grow Girl! Plant and Pursue the Power of You*

Reading through "Strong Girls" infused me with fresh faith and a holy fire to believe God has more for me in this next phase of my journey (and I'm all grown up). :) I loved this book. Girls, read this book. Soak it in. Do what it says. Engage your faith. And you will most definitely change the world.

Susie Larson
Bestselling Author, National Speaker and Talk Radio Host of *Susie Larson Live!*

ENCOURAGE THE GIRLS AROUND YOU

Share This Book

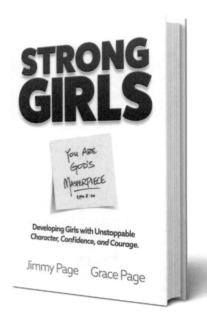

Retail: $19.95

SPECIAL QUANTITY DISCOUNTS

Quantities	Price per book (plus S & H)
5 - 9 Books	$17.95
10 - 49 Books	$16.95
50 - 99 Books	$15.95
100 - 249 Books	$13.95
250+ Books	$11.95

TO PLACE AN ORDER, CONTACT:
orderbooks@BeAStrongGirl.com
www.BeAStrongGirl.com

BOOK A SPEAKER

Want more from the Strong Girls experience?

Grace and Jimmy travel the country and speak at conferences, events, churches, colleges, camps, retreats, ministries, and schools sharing the Strong Girls message.

They do keynotes, workshops, and panel discussions and will be a perfect addition for your group!

Grace and Jimmy openly and authentically share their journey as Dad and Daughter and reveal insights you can only get in person.

If you're looking to spark a movement of *Strong Girls* in your community, book them now!

Email speak@BeAStrongGirl.com today!

DEDICATION

We dedicate
this book to every
generation of
STRONG GIRLS
who are determined
to love **JESUS**
and become
everything
they're
CREATED
to be!

CONTENTS

NTENTS

WELCOME TO THE STRONG GIRLS COMMUNITY.

I'm so excited to have y'all join Strong Girls!

It's a positive place of encouragement where you can discover your true character, confidence and courage in the Lord!

Make sure to scan the QR code below and join!

I will be adding more content to keep you growing! And, you will be able to add your own Post-its with principles and stories to encourage others in the community.

You will get access to videos from me to further explain the truth and connect you to the growing community of Strong Girls!

Together we will become the next gen world-changers!

Grace Page
@BeAStrongGirl37

HEY STRONG GIRLS!

Grace and I have had a special relationship as Daughter and Dad from the day the doctors told her mom and I we were having a girl.

With three older brothers, we knew she'd be tough and that was clear from day 1. But make no mistake, she was "all girl".

We captured her combination of strength and sass in the one word – spirited. When she was little, she didn't like that word very much, but I knew when God eventually got a hold of her, she would be a force for God and good. That has proven to be true.

After a few years of bumps and bruises, watching God create His masterpiece in Grace and work all things together for the good of those who love Him has brought healing and joy!

And now, we've watched Grace become a beautiful young woman of God who is helping other girls – from athletes to artists – become Strong Girls with unstoppable character, confidence, and courage.

God is faithful to turn our trials into testimonies. And we thank Him for the ups and downs, the cheers and tears, and now the influence and impact that Strong Girls is having on girls around the world.

Jimmy Page

PS. Grace is more spirited today than ever!

INTRODUCTION

There's never been a better time to be a girl than right now.

But that doesn't mean it's always easy, right?

There are so many voices competing for your attention to tell you who you are, what's important, and how you should act. Each voice says something different.

Family, friends, teachers, classmates, coaches, and teammates all play an important role in helping you discover who you're made to become.

Sometimes they bring out your best, and other times they pressure you to act in ways that just aren't you. Sometimes these voices make you better; other times, they make you less than you're made to be.

You may face pressure to be just like everybody else, whether it's at school, in your neighborhood, on your teams or clubs, you name it. You may face pressure to do things you know are wrong or just not best for you. And now, there's even pressure that creates confusion about what it means to be a girl.

No wonder you sometimes feel so much anxiety and uncertainty.

The good news is this – the more clearly you hear God's voice, the easier it is to see His design and plan for your life, and the more clear and confident you become.

To hear this voice, spend time getting to know Jesus. He is your shepherd and is always there, ready to guide you on the right path. That still, small voice within you quiets the noise from all the outside voices, tells you the truth, and reminds you of who God has made you to be.

In this book, we show you how to become a *Strong Girl* with unstoppable character, confidence, and courage. And we help you help others do the same.

Strong Girls is a simple, powerful, and proven process to help girls become everything they're made to be. It does all this and more:

- It makes the truth of God's Word "sticky" and easy to remember.

- It shares God's unique design for girls – beauty, brains, brawn, and brilliance.

- It makes conversations with others easy, so you know you're not alone.

- It uncovers the negative tactics and lies of the enemy and helps you win.

- It points you to the truth from the One who created you and knows you best.

- It keeps these truths in plain sight to remind you who you are throughout the day.

Strong Girls are made for more.

So let's get started on your journey to become a Strong Girl by developing the character, confidence, and courage you need to live your best life!

A life of purpose, joy, and possibility is waiting for you!

Like every **GOOD STORY,** there are **UPS AND DOWNS,** good times and bad, twists and turns...

The
Strong Girls
STORY

Like every good story, there are ups and downs, good times and bad, some twists and turns, things you didn't expect, and in the end, a ton of growth and lessons learned. The *Strong Girls* story is all that and more.

THE MOVE

The idea for *Strong Girls* was born in 2018 right after we moved from Maryland to Colorado and uprooted the life we all knew. For 20 years we had the same house, same town, same community. We knew people, and people knew us. We had a tremendous support system with church, family, and friends.

> ## *We knew the roads and had relationships everywhere.*

After relocating, we found ourselves in a new and unfamiliar environment. This was exciting in some ways, but challenging in others. In Maryland, we ran into people we knew all the time. But now we were anonymous.

Grace had the hardest transition because she not only left the comforts and connections of home, but also her childhood memories. Her brother and best friend John would head off to college across the country only two short months after the move to Colorado, preventing them from establishing a "new normal" here. She was lonely. And not having her brother by her side was an enormous loss.

Think about it – new state, new home, new school, no friends, all her brothers gone. Now that's a tough challenge for anyone, especially a teenager.

We knew it would be hardest on her.

And it was.

That's when God planted the seeds for *Strong Girls*.

Her Mom and I wanted her to connect with a local Christian youth organization so she could find friends from families that shared our values. We sent her to a week-long camp in the mountains late in the summer right before school was to begin, hoping she would make friends with girls she would then see in school.

She begged us not to send her.

She cried harder than we had ever witnessed as we dropped her off at the bus. She didn't want to go. It broke our hearts, but we believed it was best for her.

She was so far out of her
COMFORT ZONE,
and it shook her up.

During the week she was gone, I started writing encouraging notes on Post-its and put them on her bathroom and bedroom mirrors. It was a colorful display.

I hoped it would show her how much we missed her and remind her of important truths about who she was and how much God loved her.

She slept for three days when she got back.

She said she cried every day at camp. It broke our hearts to hear. But she also had made connections with a few girls she would see in class when school started. We hoped that would help her make a smoother transition.

NEW SCHOOL - NEW FRIENDS

When no one knows you or your family, it's easy to get confused about who you really are. Going with the flow to fit in is easy. Peer pressure is intense. And it feels good to be liked, especially when you've lost all your structure and security.

High School is always a time of discovery when you decide who and what kind of person you are going to be. Without friends and neighbors and coaches around who know you and your family – and what you stand for

– it's easy to get swept up and do what everybody else is doing.

Grace no longer had her brother at home as her compass and anchor. She lost that trusted voice that would always point her back to what was true and right.

New friends became super important and influential. Unfortunately, this wasn't always a good thing. And the "not-so-good" friends' voices became way louder for Grace than the "good" ones.

Grace was always strong-willed. I liked to refer to her as Spirited. But, I knew when God got ahold of this girl, she would do amazing things for His Kingdom. As time went on, that seemed more like a wish than a certainty.

She lost that **TRUSTED VOICE** *that would always point her back to what was* **TRUE** *and right.*

THE REBELLION

The next 2½ years were hard on everybody.

Filled with disrespect and defiance, many of our conversations in the home got heated as we tried to set boundaries and raise the standard for her behavior and decisions.

Our goal was to protect her from destructive decisions and shape her into the young, virtuous woman we knew she could be.

We had built a strong identity around faith and family. We had a "go against the flow" mentality. No matter what everyone else was doing, we simply would not take part if it didn't meet our standards. After all, "We are Pages."

Grace saw all our boundaries as rules that kept her from having fun when we knew they were designed to keep her free. Her friends never missed an opportunity to tell her how "strict" we were and that she should be able to do whatever she wanted.

This led to secrets, hiding, and lying. It also led to more conflict and contentious conversations with high emotion.

It was a roller-coaster, to say the least. She wanted to do what most of her friends were doing. She wanted to be popular and liked and was willing to compromise to get it.

We had virtually no support in the community because we didn't know anybody and had no history.

This funny, goofy, spirited little girl had become someone that we didn't even recognize. She pushed all our limits and crossed just about every boundary we set for her benefit and blessing.

Our relationship was always special, but it had grown cold and distant. It was a challenging and disappointing time. Grace was trying to fill the emptiness she was feeling on the inside with friends, boys, and independence.

At the worst of it, just a couple of months before her 18th birthday, she was threatening to leave our home and go stay at a friend's house. She was determined to gain her independence from all our rules and restrictions that were, as she liked to say, "choking" her.

In a last-ditch effort to keep her under our roof, we made a deal with her. If she wanted the freedom to make all her own decisions, she could, but she would have to start paying for it. That meant she'd have to pay for her car, insurance, gas, and phone; all I asked in return was that she kept a reasonable curfew so we wouldn't be up all night worrying about her. Part of our "deal" was also that she would pay for college. She agreed. She probably didn't realize exactly what that meant.

THE RETURN

All the while, I kept putting notes on her mirrors with truth and encouragement, believing that God would eventually break through to her and set her free from her choices. It turns out that had a cumulative effect. We did our best to stay positive and encouraging.

We kept showing up for everything to support her – lacrosse games, school stuff, you name it. During the rebellion, God gave Grace a couple of really good friends who were willing to speak the truth to her along the way. They defended her Mom and me and challenged her to make better decisions.

After a while, the weight of poor decisions finally added up.

The friends she thought would make her feel like she belonged never did.

The boys she thought would treat her right and make her feel special never did.

Life with few limits wasn't so great after all.

She realized that it never feels good to do the wrong thing. The freedom and independence she wanted so much led to less freedom and more guilt and disappointment. She didn't like the person she had become very much and missed the safety and security of home.

But as she matured and started spending more time with friends who loved Jesus and brought her life, the more she appreciated her Mom and me. She saw the contrast.

We started seeing signs of the "old" Grace again as she realized just how difficult she had been. To be honest, we weren't sure if this was for real because she had been so hot and cold for the last two years. Over time, we realized this was a real return. More consistency over time had started to rebuild trust.

We felt a tremendous sense of relief.

We knew the road to restoration would take time and it would be a process for her to fully mature.

We were surprised when she mentioned her desire to attend a Christian college. As her decision eventually settled in on Liberty University (LU) we were thrilled. Her brother John had one more year there, so her transition would be relatively easy. We knew God would restore their closeness and it would bless Grace. And, because we were so encouraged by her transformation of attitude, perspective, and behavior, we decided to pay for it. We wanted to model what unconditional love and grace looked like tangibly.

The culture at Liberty was exactly what Grace needed to help her continue to grow in her faith and character.

THE REVIVAL

During the hardest moments, her Mom and I were determined to never give up. We held on tight to the masterpiece we knew she would become when she surrendered to Jesus.

At LU, Grace found herself immersed in an environment that had the same standards we had established and lived out at home. Girls just like her were genuinely pursuing God and a different life. They had weekly worship and teaching with everybody who lived on campus and it rekindled her spirit.

Now, was everybody at LU perfect? Far from it. But many were authentic. Life in Christ is not about perfection, it's about direction. And Grace's direction was getting reoriented toward true north.

Life in Christ is not about **PERFECTION,** *it's about* **DIRECTION.**

We have always been a grace & freedom family, believing that Jesus came to set us free from sin and death so that we could live an abundant life – a rich, satisfying, make-a-difference kind of life. We rejected the legalism of behavior modification, where you have to be "good enough" to earn God's love and favor; that's pure nonsense. God loves us unconditionally and wants us to become everything He's made us to be. God's kindness leads to repentance.

We saw a dramatic change of heart in Grace. It was softer, less judgmental, more forgiving, and grateful. She became more hopeful again. More positive and optimistic. And all the wild, emotional mood swings and combative conversations were gone.

It was truly a miracle.

She was alive again in Christ – studying the Bible, connected with a small group, and growing in her faith. She had truly surrendered her life to Christ.

THE HEALING

Becoming your best is a never-ending process. It's a process involving the mind, body, and spirit. Sometimes you need healing before you can truly get strong.

Grace worked hard to win the mental game. She still was struggling with holding on to past mistakes. The enemy tried to weigh her down with the past, distract her with the challenges of the present, and fill her with anxiety and worry for the future. She struggled with insecurity, fear, and feelings of not being good enough. So she fought.

She called me and asked me how to stop the lies. I reminded her of all the truth from God's Word. I reminded her of all the post-it notes she still had on her mirrors. Grace needed to get back on offense if she was going to win. This would become a daily battle, but I knew it was one she could and must win if she were to live with peace and joy.

Grace **NEEDED** *to get back on* **OFFENSE** *if she was going to* **WIN.**

Grace saw it. And then she worked hard to stop the doom loop of negative, destructive thinking. In the end, she started to consistently replace the lies with the truth and it brought a revival in her mind, emotions, and spirit. She experienced true healing, but it didn't happen overnight.

Then she got healthy...and strong. And she put in the work.

Grace also knew that her physical health affected her mental and emotional stability. As she took more responsibility for decisions with food, working out, and sleep, everything got better fast. The mental clarity, energy, and positive mood was noticeable to her and others. She became vibrantly alive from the inside out.

CHARACTER - CONFIDENCE - COURAGE

To see Grace growing and thriving in all aspects of life is an answer to prayer. It's a real demonstration of the power of God and a testimony that God has a beautiful plan and never wastes trials and challenges.

Her character was forged in the fire. And while there were plenty of moments where everybody wanted to just quit, God carried us until we could overcome.

She has become confident in who she is and what she believes.

She has become courageous in living a life that honors Jesus, regardless of the pressure or challenges or obstacles along the path.

Hey, and everybody knows it will never be perfect! We are all a work in progress. But God will be faithful to complete this masterpiece.

Of that, we are sure.

Her CHARACTER *was forged in the* FIRE.

God will

FORGE

in you

UNSTOPPABLE

character,

confidence,

and

courage

The
PROMISE

The *Strong Girls* Promise is this – *when you plant the truth of God's Word in the hearts of girls, and keep it front and center, The Creator will produce young ladies with unstoppable character, confidence, and courage.*

That's not really just our promise, that's God's promise. God is faithful to complete what He starts. He never leaves a masterpiece unfinished. And that is wonderful news.

No matter how messy it may look along the way, ultimately it will be truly magnificent.

Character, confidence, and courage make girls strong. We call them *The Core.*

They are like a cord of three strands and are not easily broken. As each of those three pieces grows, it makes girls unstoppable!

Character forms the foundation and without it, all the confidence and courage in the world are worthless. But with godly character, confidence and courage have world-changing value.

THE RESULT

While this journey will be far from perfect, filled with wins and losses, ups and downs, triumphs and setbacks, cheers and tears, keep your head up and stay the course.

You experience a life of
PURPOSE and BELONGING,
one that matters and makes a
DIFFERENCE
for others.

Here are some practical characteristics of *Strong Girls*.

Strong Girls:

1. Have a strong and growing identity in Christ.

2. Set big goals and pursue them with passion.

3. Have a positive, optimistic mindset.

4. Use challenges and obstacles to make them better.

5. Enjoy vibrant mental, physical, and emotional health.

6. Experience uplifting and satisfying relationships.

7. Make a difference.

Why do the 3 components of *The Core* matter so much? Because when you act with character, confidence, and courage, you live with incredible freedom, and you flourish. You become everything you're made to be. You make fewer mistakes and live with fewer regrets.

Your life becomes faithful, fulfilling, and fruitful. You live a life you're proud of. You experience a life of purpose and belonging, one that matters and makes a difference for others. And you bear much fruit.

This is the abundant life that Jesus told you was yours for the taking! (John 10:10) And we all want a life of love, joy, and peace.

Character, confidence, and courage. These are the core components of a high-impact life in Christ. The combination of these turns victims into heroes.

Strong Girls are created to be world-changers. *Strong Girls* are simply happier and healthier.

We promise that if you do the work, God will forge in you unstoppable character, confidence, and courage.

Do the work and expect God to transform you into everything you're made to be!

The **CORE** of Strong Girls will create more clarity, purpose, and **POWER FOR LIFE.**

The
CORE

CHARACTER, CONFIDENCE, AND COURAGE

Remember the *Strong Girls* promise – *when you plant the truth of God's Word in the hearts of girls, and keep it front and center, The Creator will produce young ladies with unstoppable character, confidence, and courage.*

When Grace was about twelve, we went vacationing in Lake Placid, NY, one of her favorite places to visit. Besides playing in a lacrosse tournament, we went cliff jumping. It was always a highlight of the trip.

There were three different heights to jump from and the highest jump had some serious risks. It was about 50 feet high; that was enough to stop most from attempting it.

Plus, you had to get a running start, plant your foot in an exact spot close to the edge, jump far enough to clear a tree jutting out and rocks below, but not too far because you'd hit the shallow water. No one wanted to hit trees, rocks, or the bottom of the river.

Sound fun?

No one wanted to hit **TREES, ROCKS,** *or the bottom of the* **RIVER.**

Well, for Grace, she was determined to do it. She had a tenacious spirit. Her character was full of faith, hope, and fortitude, but she may have been still developing wisdom! She was confident that she was athletic enough to pull it off. The only thing left was courage.

It took her almost twenty minutes to follow my lead off the rocks, but she trusted me and saw others jump successfully. Finally, she summoned enough courage to do it.

It was exhilarating.

And in that moment, I knew she was going to be a *Strong Girl*.

Let's take a closer look at these three core components of *Strong Girls*.

CHARACTER

CONFIDENCE

COURAGE

CHARACTER - WHO YOU TRULY ARE.

The simplest and most powerful definition of character is this – **character is who you truly are.**

Character forms the foundation of your life.

The foundation is the starting point for every house that has ever been built. The more level and solid and deep that foundation, the more secure and tall and beautiful the house can be. The building won't last very long if the foundation cracks or if it's built on sand.

Integrity and virtue make up two key parts of character.

Integrity means consistently living up to good moral principles. It means that you say what you mean and you do what you say. There is a consistency between your beliefs, values, attitudes, words, and actions. When you have integrity, you are truthful and trustworthy; you can be counted on to do the right thing regardless of the situation or the consequences.

Virtues are the good moral practices that a person of integrity strives to live by. They are behaviors and actions of moral excellence. As you will learn in chapter 6, virtues are principles in action like honesty, courage, humility, kindness, modesty, self-control, and generosity.

Your character is formed by what you believe, what you say, and what you do.

How you act doesn't change based on who you're with or the situation you're facing. Character means doing what you say you will do and keeping your commitments.

The most common ways you might compromise your character are by hiding, lying, keeping secrets, making excuses, and taking shortcuts. Growing virtues like honesty, taking responsibility, and grit help grow your character and stop compromise.

There are many things you can do to hurt your character:

1. Gossiping or talking about others behind their back.

2. Refusing to defend someone who needs your help.

3. Compromising your standards to be popular.

4. Acting differently depending on who you're with.

5. Refusing to take responsibility or ask for forgiveness when necessary.

Character is **BUILT** *on the foundation of* **KNOWING** *what is right and* **DOING** *it.*

The list is endless, but you get the idea.

When you have solid character – integrity and virtue – you become unshakable and secure.

Character is built on the foundation of knowing what is right and doing it. The Bible is full of wisdom and truth you can count on. It's always true regardless of what the culture says is right or wrong. God's principles are timeless and do not change depending on what's new and trendy.

Character means you will not compromise your values and beliefs. It serves as the foundation on which the others are built. Knowing who God is, who you are, what you stand for, and what you do and don't do – these things make you strong.

Character is doing what is good and right:

- even when no one is looking.

- even when you're under pressure from others.

- no matter what other people will say.

- no matter how it turns ou.

It always feels good to do the good and right thing. Holding to a high moral standard may not make you popular, but it pleases God. When you consistently do the good and right thing, you learn you can trust God and yourself no matter what situation you find yourself in.

Here are the top 3 actions to build your character:

1. **Build your life on God's truth, not "your" truth.** Jesus said I am The Way, The Truth, and The Life. All truth lives in the person of Jesus. The Bible and the life of Christ have revealed timeless truth. When you stay tight to Jesus, you get truth and wisdom for life. (John 14:6)

2. **Be the real you no matter who you're with.** When you don't change how you act or behave depending on who you're with, or where you are, that's a sign of integrity. (2 Cor. 5:17)

3. **Do the right thing no matter what.** This is simple, but not easy. When you get in the habit of doing the right thing even when it's hard, or when no one else would know, and even no matter how it turns out, that is a sign you have excellent character. (Joshua 1:9, Proverbs 10:9, Galatians 6:9)

Having good moral character is more valuable than great riches.

Ultimately, your quest for character is about being transformed into the likeness of Christ – becoming more and more like Jesus. It's a process. It takes time. It's not about perfection, it's about progress.

KEY TRUTHS

1. Character forms the foundation of your life.

2. Character is doing what is good and right, no matter what.

3. Your character is revealed through what you believe, say, and do.

Add your own thoughts and observations:

_____

_____

_____

_____

KEY VERSES

1. **Do Good** – Titus 2:7-8
2. **Act Justly** – Micah 6:8
3. **A Good Name** – Proverbs 22:1
4. **Set the Example** – 1 Timothy 4:12
5. **Goodness & Godliness** – 2 Peter 1:5-7
6. **Walk in Integrity** – Proverbs 10:9
7. **Be Fruitful** – Galatians 5:22-23
8. **God Upholds You**– Psalm 41:12
9. **Fear the Lord** – Proverbs 1:7
10. **Know the Truth** – John 8:31-32

CONFIDENCE - EXTREME BELIEF, CERTAINTY AND TRUST

The simplest and most powerful definition of confidence is this – **confidence is extreme belief, certainty, and trust.**

Confidence empowers you to live your dreams and make a difference.

Building confidence requires a solid foundation of character and trust. Trust is built on consistent behavior, developing the certainty that you can count on someone or something.

Confidence comes from character, capability, and keeping your commitments to yourself and others. You cannot have confidence if you don't keep your promises to yourself first and then to others.

It also comes from having a track record of success. Confidence is built on overwhelming evidence. Doing what you say you will do builds your own confidence and others' confidence in you.

There are many things that chip away at your confidence. Here are some practical examples that can weaken your confidence:

1. Breaking promises to yourself or others.

2. Believing the lies and self-sabotaging thoughts about yourself.

3. Shrinking back from a challenge or obstacle.

4. Dwelling on past failures.

5. Playing it safe and not trying new things.

The list is endless, but you get the idea.

Everyone has setbacks, but failure should never define you. All these things can be corrected. Each one gives you an opportunity to get right back in the game and do it right the next time. You are just one decision and action away from getting going in the right direction again.

Everyone has **SETBACKS,** *but* **FAILURE** *should never* **DEFINE** *you.*

You don't find confidence in the "power of positive thinking", but in the power of God's word.

While it's very true that a positive mindset matters, unless you fill that mindset with the principles of God's truth, it lacks lasting power. The principles, promises, and wisdom in God's Word are trustworthy.

That's why every "post-it" note given to Grace had a true, sticky statement tied to a scripture with timeless truth.

Winning the mental game of confidence is important. Some create "mantras" like "I got this" to help them overcome challenges, but a more powerful statement might be "Nothing is impossible with God." Both may be helpful, but only one places their confidence in God.

When trying to overcome overwhelming pressure, fear, and anxiety, we find another example. Using mantras like "I'm better under pressure" or "No pressure, No diamonds" is super helpful. Tying them to passages of scripture makes them powerful. Statements like "Bring it on!" or "Obstacles make me stronger" when connected to scripture found in James 1 give you an expectation that every trial is a good thing, meant to benefit you and make you better. How much confidence might this generate?

Building true confidence does not solely rely on affirmations, but also on evidence. When you accumulate wins, you empower yourself for every challenge.

Strong Girls have an unshakeable confidence because you have the certainty of God's love, power, and goodness no matter what life brings. You can "laugh at your problems" and be excited about the future because God is with you wherever you go.

You can be confident in God even when you are at your weakest point.

Here are the top 3 actions to build your confidence:

1. **Do what you say you will do.** If you make commitments to God or promises to yourself, keep them. If you've set a standard for how you will behave, or your family has certain expectations, meet those expectations. Keep your commitments even when you don't feel like it. Don't make excuses or compromise. (Eccl. 5:4, Psalm 15:4, Matthew 5:37)

2. **Get comfortable being uncomfortable.** When you're striving to be everything you're made to be, you will get comfortable doing things differently from most. Getting outside your comfort zone makes you stretch and grow. (Matthew 14:28-29, Hebrews 11:8)

3. **Do hard things.** Real confidence comes from taking risks and doing hard things. It makes you test your limits and become more capable. Taking the easy way never makes you better. Doing hard things is soul-satisfying and empowering. The narrow road is the hard road, and it leads to life. (2 Corinthians 6:4-9, Acts 20:22-23)

> You can *"LAUGH at your problems"* and be **EXCITED** about the **FUTURE** because God is with you wherever you go.

When you build your confidence on the timeless truth of God's Word – His unconditional love, limitless grace, and ultimate goodness – you live with certainty, power, and joy.

Ultimately, your confidence comes from trusting God and taking actions consistent with who you are in Christ. And this *Strong Girls* journey is a masterful partnership of God's power and your action!

KEY TRUTHS

1. Confidence is built on extreme trust in God and yourself.

2. Building confidence requires getting outside your comfort zone.

3. Confidence is forged by bouncing back from setbacks.

Add your own thoughts and observations:

_____

_____

_____

_____

KEY VERSES

1. **All Things** – Philippians 4:13
2. **Yes Means Yes** – Matthew 5:37
3. **Keep Your Word** – Ecclesiastes 5:4
4. **Faith > Fear** – Matthew 14:28-29
5. **Fear the Lord** – Proverbs 9:10
6. **Confidence In Christ** – 2 Corinthians 3:4-5
7. **Ask God** – 1 John 5:14
8. **Protection** – Proverbs 3:26
9. **In Uncertain Times** – Hebrews 11:8
10. **Hardships Help** – Acts 20:22-23

COURAGE – TAKING ACTION IN THE FACE OF FEAR.

The simplest and most powerful definition of courage is this – *taking action in the face of fear.*

Courage is the ability to exercise your confidence and character. Courage is putting those two things into action in specific situations you face. Courage isn't the absence of fear. It's taking action even though you are afraid.

Courage is when you stand up in the face of adversity or challenge and do the right thing, regardless of potential negative consequences. Courage is when you're willing to stand alone. Courage is when you do the right thing for the right reasons.

There is often a cost that comes with living a life of courage. But the rewards are worth it.

Fear prevents most people from going for it in life. It also stops most from speaking up or standing up for what they believe. It's amazing how paralyzing fear can be.

There are many things that keep you from living courageously:

1. Fear of failure or looking foolish.

2. Fear of standing alone and not being supported.

3. Fear of standing out and being rejected.

4. Fear of being judged or misunderstood.

5. Fear of being criticized or called names.

The list is endless, but you get the idea.

The Bible has daily encouragement to be courageous and conquer your fears.

Fear is the obstacle to an amazing life. To have an amazing life, the road leads straight through fear. The obstacle is the way.

Here are the top 3 actions to be courageous:

1. **Take Risks.** Be willing to step out in faith when you feel compelled to do so. Courage means that you take action, even though you are afraid. Do it afraid. God will step in and give you the words and strength that you need when you're doing the right thing, pursuing audacious goals, or helping someone in need. (Hebrews 11:6)

2. **Go against the flow.** Peer pressure is a very intense deal. The pressure to do what everybody else is doing, or wearing, or saying can cause enough fear to make you compromise and conform. *Strong Girls* are called to obey God and go against the flow. They've been set apart. When you take on the go against the flow mindset, it makes you stronger. (Romans 12:1-2)

3. **Take a Stand!** There are three components of taking a stand – *stand up* for what you believe, what's true, and what's right, *stand against* what's evil, wrong, and unfair, and *stand with* those who are the least, last, and left out. This requires empathy and compassion, as well as the willingness to conquer your fears. (Joshua 1:9, Ephesians 6:13, Micah 6:8)

Courage is the culmination of your character and confidence in God. It takes time to develop it, but it leads to a life of mission and meaning.

These 3 core components are forged over time. When you put your beliefs and values into action, all three grow and get stronger.

Strong Girls develop incredible core strength that makes you unstoppable in life.

KEY TRUTHS

1.   Courage is acting in the face of fear.

2.   Courage means moving in God's power.

3.   Courage requires trusting God completely.

Add your own thoughts and observations:

_____

_____

_____

_____

KEY VERSES

1.   **Strong & Courageous** – Joshua 1:9
2.   **Against the Flow** – Romans 12:1-2
3.   **Be on Guard** – 1 Corinthians 16:13
4.   **Stand your Ground** – Ephesians 6:13
5.   **Love Justice** – Micah 6:8
6.   **Big Faith** – Hebrews 11:6
7.   **Walk in Power** – 2 Timothy 1:7
8.   **God is For You** – Romans 8:31
9.   **Bold as a Lion** – Proverbs 28:1
10. **No Fear** – Isaiah 41:10
11. **God Overcomes** – John 16:33

The
Strong Girls
PROCESS
was
FORGED
in the fire of
REAL-LIFE
challenges and
celebrations.

The
PROCESS

The *Strong Girls* **process** was forged in the fire of real-life challenges and celebrations.

We know it works because it's worked for us over several years of trial and error.

Through our own experience and the encouragement of countless others, we now get to share the simple three-step process of building character, confidence, and courage.

SEE IT - STOP IT - START IT

The see it, stop it, start it formula for growth is the "secret sauce" of *Strong Girls*. It's a simple and powerful way to examine your life, decide, and take action to stop destructive behavior and start consistent behaviors that lead to life.

1. **SEE IT** – be honest as you look for areas of your life that need to get better and "see it".

2. **STOP IT** – commit to one thing you can stop doing that is preventing you from improving.

3. **START IT** – commit to one thing to start doing consistently that will help you be your best.

At first glance you may think, "that's it?" Yep. That's the genius of almost every process that works – it's simple and intuitive.

Before you can change anything or make it better, you must be able to see the gap between where you are and where you want to be. You must see the opportunities for growth between who you currently are and who you are capable of being.

This three-step process works for everybody if you commit to it. And when you get a little practice, this will become second nature and help you level-up every area of your life.

The
SEE IT,
STOP IT,
START IT
formula for growth is the
"SECRET SAUCE"
of Strong Girls.

THE POWER OF THE POST-IT

Putting Post-its on Grace's mirrors became an easy way to get positive, powerful messages of truth in front of her in her everyday environment.

I wanted the truth to be short and sweet. And I always wanted to tie the short message to a bible verse reference so 1, she knew where the truth came from, and 2, she could open her bible and find the verse herself. I figured that might lead to her reading more and thought that would always be a good thing.

I also wanted the messages to be "sticky" so she would remember them.

The limited space took the pressure off from having to write a long, eloquent message on a note card and became something she could "move" so it could easily go with her and stay front-and-center.

She would take them off her bathroom mirror and put it on her school notebook, her lacrosse locker, or on her car dashboard. That way, the post-it messages ended up as reminders for her, no matter where she was or what she was doing.

KEEP IT SIMPLE & STAY POSITIVE

I had to resist the urge to make it more complicated and write too much on the post-it. Instead, I knew I had to keep it simple and make every message a positive one.

I wanted to make sure it was something she would look forward to and not something she would grow to dread. No negative messages ever! Stay positive.

STRENGTH TRAINING

When you get to the 37 days of strength training in chapter 7, you will see a Post-it and sticky statement with the verse that we used. Next is a story from Grace and a short teaching on the *Strong Girls* principle.

Things like "You are God's Masterpiece," "No Pressure, No Diamonds," "God is for You," "Keep Your Head Up," "Be a Warrior, Not a Whiner," and more will be a source of easy-to-remember truth to lift and encourage.

Finally, we will walk you through the SEE IT – STOP IT – START IT process to make you strong.

It's as simple as that.

STRONG GIRLS WORKS

Strong Girls is contagious. And it works.

You can go through the book by yourself, with your teammates or classmates, with your small group, or with your parents.

Moms and Dads love how easy it is to drop some encouragement to their daughters and they're amazed at how it opens up authentic conversations.

It's perfect for youth groups and accountability groups for girls. Imagine the encouragement you might give someone just at the time they need it.

Strong Girls is timeless and powerful. It doesn't change with changing times or winds of the culture because it's built on the unchanging Word of God.

The process takes a little time, but the results are worth it. This process works!

LET'S GET STARTED

As you get started, it's helpful to know the strategies of the enemy and God's perfect design.

Ready?

Let's go!

DEMOLISH THE LIES WITH TRUTH!

(2 Cor. 10:4-5)

If God is **FOR YOU,** who can be **AGAINST** you?

The
*ENEMY'S
STRATEGY*

Some girls are unaware that they have an enemy. But in the earliest days following Creation, we read the story of Adam and Eve being tempted by the "serpent" to disobey God. As the story unfolds, we learn the enemy was successful in getting Eve, then Adam, to eat from the tree of the knowledge of good and evil; that was the only tree God told them was off limits. They gave in to the temptation and sin entered the world.

You have an enemy and his purpose is to interfere with your relationship with Jesus, stop you from enjoying life, and keep you all tied up. Jesus came to set you free, give you a life of abundance, and offer you the free gift of eternal life. Satan – your enemy – prowls around like a lion looking for someone to devour. He is a thief, a liar, and an accuser.

There is a spiritual battle going on all around us and we need to have "eyes to see it" and the strategy to fight it.

Your enemy works hard to make you think he doesn't exist, so you won't be prepared to fight against his schemes and tricks to ruin your life and make you miserable. He wants to keep you insecure, anxious, and afraid. He wants you lonely and depressed.

But the good news is this – "The one who is in you is greater than the one who is in the world." (1 John 4:4) God is for you, so who cares who's against you. And even though you will face temptation to do the wrong thing, God always provides you with a way out.

So let's talk a little about the enemy's strategies so you can be ready to win!

1.   **The enemy controls you through thoughts and emotions.** This is his #1 strategy. The enemy can and will use any words you say against you. That's why you must be careful what you say – especially if it's negative or self-defeating. Your thoughts have a direct impact on your emotions. If you are negative, pessimistic, self-critical, complaining, or gossiping, the enemy *turns all*

those thoughts into emotions like fear, anxiety, insecurity, anger, jealousy, discouragement, and loneliness. When you win this battle, you win almost every other battle.

2. **The enemy controls you through the past, present, and future.** If he can keep you weighed down, distracted, and worried, he can rob you of freedom and life. He is great at reminding you of past mistakes and weighing you down with the emotions of guilt and shame. He keeps you distracted in the present with busyness, selfishness, and temptations of fitting in, being liked, or wasting time on social media. And he keeps you worried and anxious about the future to rob you of enjoying life right now.

3. **The enemy tempts you with the easy road.** He makes things look like God's design, but they're always a cheap imitation. Things look so good, but they always end so bad. He appeals to your lack of patience and promises pleasure right now if you will just cut a few corners and compromise who you are. God's best is never easy, and it's rarely immediate. Usually, the right way is discovered by doing hard things and it requires time.

4. **The enemy tempts you with the things of this world.** The enemy always wants to get your eyes off God and onto yourself; and it's easy most of the time because we're naturally self-centered. He tempts us to want things that are bad for us, to want more and more stuff that we don't need, and to feel important because of our success. (1 John 2:16) This means we let the flesh control us, instead of The Spirit. The worst part is when you give in, you feel horrible. God's ways are always best; you just need to believe it and choose to do it God's way.

In his best-selling book, The Garden, my co-author and friend Jon Gordon reveals the 5 D's the devil uses to defeat us – *doubt, distortion, discouragement, distraction, and division.*

The devil wants to defeat you.

He wants to wound you and make you feel bad about yourself. He wants you to doubt God's love for you. He wants you to feel all alone. He uses guilt and shame to silence you and make you feel small. He sure doesn't want you to shine brightly for God.

But God has unique plans for you and He's way more powerful than the enemy.

God has given you everything you need to stand against the enemy. You are powerful when you use those weapons like prayer and God's Word. The truth always defeats lies.

You must overwhelm the lies with the truth found in the Bible. God's Truth is the antidote to the lies. When the enemy tempted Jesus following his 40 days in the wilderness – when He was hungry, tired, and weak – Jesus answered every single time with "it is written..." In other words, "God says..." (Matthew 4:1-11)

> *You must*
> # OVERWHELM
> *the lies with the*
> # TRUTH
> *found in the Bible.*

The enemy is relentless, so you must be more relentless. You can and must win the daily battle for your mind. When you allow a little negativity, it grows; that's why every thought matters. When you win this fight, it feels really, really good.

Be Ready.

***Strong Girls* know the enemy and are ready for his schemes and strategies.** You can see them coming a mile away. The enemy lies, cheats, and steals. And he will try to get you to do the same. He wants to keep you in bondage because God wants you completely FREE!

He wants to make you weak and powerless.

God wants to make you strong and powerful as you believe the truth and put your trust in Him.

God never condemns you.

When He forgives, He forgets it and so should you.

If God is for you, who can be against you.

No weapon formed against you will prosper.

Greater is He who is in you than he who is in the world.

You have not received a spirit of fear, but of love, power, and a sound mind.

Where the Spirit of the Lord is there is freedom.

Whom the Son sets free is free indeed.

When you are weak, God is strong.

Strong Girls are ready to fight and win.

KEY TRUTHS

1. You have an enemy.

2. God is greater than your enemy.

3. God's armor protects you from the enemy.

Add your own thoughts and observations:

_____

_____

_____

_____

KEY VERSES

1. **The enemy prowls** – 1 Peter 5:8
2. **He schemes** – Ephesians 6:11
3. **He lies** – John 8:44
4. **He condemns** – Revelation 12:10
5. **He tempts** – Matthew 4:1-11
6. **He tempts again** – 1 John 2:16
7. **He divides** – Ephesians 6:12
8. **God is Greater** – 1 John 4:4
9. **New Weapons** – 2 Corinthians 10:4
10. **Escape temptation** – 1 Corinthians 10:13
11. **God's Armor** – Ephesians 6:10-13
12. **No Weapon or Accusation** – Isaiah 54:17
13. **God is for you** – Romans 8:31
14. **No Fear** – 2 Timothy 1:7
15. **You can overcome** – Romans 8:37
16. **Strong in Weakness** – 2 Corinthians 12:10
17. **Nothing can separate** – Romans 8:38-39
18. **Jesus sets you free** – Galatians 5:1

You ARE
FEARFULLY
AND
WONDERFULLY
MADE.

(Psalm 139:13-14)

All of **US**
are made
in the
IMAGE of
GOD.

GOD'S
DESIGN

God is the Creator of all things, but most importantly, he's the Creator of you. Before you were even born, God knew you. He formed you in your mother's womb. And He created plans for a beautiful life for you. You are not an accident. You are important and invaluable.

God's design for girls is unique and wonderful. Genesis 1:27 says this, "So God created mankind in his own image, in the image of God He created them; male and female He created them."

All of us bear the image of God. We all represent the unique qualities of God. And while we are different, we all have equal value in God's eyes.

Obviously, girls are different from boys and thank God for that. Aside from the obvious physical and physiological differences, God has given girls and boys different primary roles and responsibilities. They complement one another as part of God's perfect design for the family.

God has revealed the stories of remarkable women in the Bible who played incredible roles in the family, community, and as instrumental parts of God's redemptive story. Women like *Ruth, Esther, Tamar, Rahab, Rebekah, Jochebed (Moses' Mom), Deborah, Mary Magdalene, Mary (Jesus' Mom), Martha, and many more.* Numerous other stories highlight the virtue, faith, and devotion of women who were unnamed. Studying each of their stories is a must.

There are four beautiful facets of God's design for girls, and all of them make girls strong – *Beauty, Brains, Brawn, and Brilliance.* Each of these facets is a unique expression of God's perfect design for girls. That's why it's important for you to uncover God's truth about each.

In this section, we will examine God's perfect design for you as a girl. God's ways are perfect. His design always brings life. The closer you get to living your life the way it's designed, the more joyful, satisfying, and meaningful it will be.

We will use these facets to help you see the truth clearly. And, we'll make these facets into targets to shoot for as you become everything God has made you to be.

The closer you get to
LIVING YOUR LIFE
*the way it's designed,
the more*

JOYFUL,

SATISFYING,
and

MEANINGFUL
it will be.

> BEAUTY
> COMES FROM THE
> INSIDE
> OUT
>
> (1 Peter 3:3-4)

BEAUTY
MADE
TO BE
VIRTUOUS

BEAUTY - MADE TO BE VIRTUOUS

When we say *Strong Girls* have Beauty, we are referring to **presence & virtue.** And that is God's design for girls.

You may have heard that "beauty is only skin deep." That means that the outer physical appearance doesn't determine who that person is on the inside. And outward beauty can't change a person's heart or character. It won't change their personality and make them a kinder person. Outward beauty also fades over time, no matter how hard you try to stay young.

You may have also heard the saying, "beauty is in the eye of the beholder." That means that each one of us will have a different idea about what is truly beautiful. What is beautiful to you may be ugly to someone else. And that's part of what makes the world a wonderful place with incredible variety.

But true human beauty is in the eye of the Creator. The one who created it all gets to define what is truly beautiful. It's up to each one of us to seek and discover what God sees as true beauty and then align our hearts with His.

External beauty of creation is easy to see. In the very first book of the Bible, Genesis, God created the heavens and the earth and everything in them. And He calls all of creation 'good.'

He gave us the stars in the sky so we would declare the greatness of God. He gave us flowers and plants and trees, the animals on the ground, sea creatures under water, and the birds of the air. He gave us mountains and valleys, lakes and rivers and oceans, and even sunshine and rain. His amazing creativity is everywhere around us for our enjoyment.

God puts the outward beauty of creation on display every day.

God designed human beauty from the inside out. God never uses external beauty to determine the beauty of a human being. And while people certainly can be attractive and beautiful, that always depends on who is judging. When God was choosing a King, He chose David because David loved God and wanted to live for Him. His brothers were more handsome, impressive, and strong, but God cares more about the inside than the outside appearance.

The presence of God in you gives you true beauty. Have you ever been around someone who became much prettier once you got to know them? People who are beautiful on the inside always appear more beautiful on the outside. The opposite is also true. Someone who is ugly on the inside (full of negativity, anger, gossip, or criticism) always becomes less pretty on the outside. It's easy to have the outward appearance of beauty and much harder to have the character qualities that make you truly beautiful. The fruit of the Spirit in you makes you beautiful.

God determines beauty based on inside qualities. Those qualities are called virtues, and every one of us can develop these virtues and become a truly beautiful person from the inside out. It's God's design – you are made to be virtuous.

We define virtues as good moral qualities. There are many virtuous qualities, all of which, when put into practice, will make you into a beautiful person.

Virtues are the ingredients that form your character.

Here is a starter list of the most commonly accepted virtues that have the most positive transformational impact on who you are as a person – *honesty, wisdom, discipline, justice, courage, humility, gratitude, generosity, positivity, curiosity, fortitude, resilience, diligence, obedience, perseverance, faith, hope, love, mercy, compassion, purity, patience, kindness, joy, contentment, and zeal.*

When you intentionally focus on developing these virtues, God makes them part of your DNA, part of who you are.

When you live out these virtues and allow the Spirit of God to lead you, you will produce what God calls fruit in your life. Fruit can be "inside" (character) and "outside" (actions).

God describes the qualities of a virtuous young woman. In Proverbs 31:10-31, God describes what the life of a virtuous woman looks like. That woman fears the Lord and is trustworthy, faithful, hardworking, wise, kind, generous, organized, strong, dignified, joyful, humble, positive, and encouraging. When others watch her, that is what they see.

You can develop all these virtues within yourself. You aren't born with them. You don't get them overnight. You develop them over time as you seek to be transformed into the image of Jesus because He is all those things perfectly. Be patient, but be intentional to focus on displaying these virtues in everyday situations.

Beauty is demonstrated in your thoughts, words, attitudes, emotions, and actions.

Sometimes you feel beautiful and other times you don't.

Sometimes you act beautifully, and other times you act ugly.

What comes out of you is really a reflection of what's happening on the inside of you. The things you say and do tell us a lot about your heart. God says your words show you what's going on in your heart. (Luke 6:45) That's a little scary, isn't it?

To be sure, it's not a bad thing to be physically beautiful; and it's also a virtue to take care of your body and appearance. That is called good stewardship, and it's a reflection of your love for the one who created you. But God just wants to make sure you spend more time cultivating the inside and less time dressing up the outside. (1 Peter 3:3-4)

Everyone can have beauty because everyone can be virtuous. You are made to be virtuous.

KEY TRUTHS

1. Beauty is in the eye of the Creator

2. Beauty comes from the inside, out.

3. The Presence of God's Spirit in you makes you beautiful.

Add your own thoughts and observations:

_____

_____

_____

_____

_____

KEY VERSES

1. **Inner Beauty** – 1 Peter 3:3-4
2. **Image Bearer** – Genesis 1:27
3. **God's Masterpiece** – Ephesians 2:10
4. **Virtuous Woman** – Proverbs 31:10-31
5. **Goodness & Godliness** – 2 Peter 1:5-7
6. **Heart / Words** – Luke 6:45
7. **God's Perspective** – 1 Samuel 16:7b
8. **God's Timing** – Ecclesiastes 3:11
9. **Fearfully Made** – Psalm 139:13-14
10. **Modest Attire** – 1 Timothy 2:9-10
11. **God's Work** – Philippians 1:6
12. **Fruitful Spirit** – Galatians 5:22-23

THINK
LIKE
JESUS

(1 Cor. 2:16)

BRAINS
MADE
TO BE WISE

BRAINS - MADE TO BE WISE

When we say *Strong Girls* have Brains, we are referring to **mindset and wisdom.** And that is God's design for girls.

When most of you think of "brains", you immediately think of being smart. And while knowledge is important and part of brains, it's a tiny part of what we mean for *Strong Girls*. For *Strong Girls*, we're talking about creating a powerful mindset based on truth and applying that truth to life.

Wisdom is way more important than being smart. You all know those friends who are super smart in school – "book smart" – but who struggle with common sense. Well, we want to be smart in school, have common sense, and be able to make wise decisions.

You already know that the Bible is the source of all truth and wisdom.

An entire book called Proverbs is devoted to wisdom for life. The Bible gives you truth to apply to your relationships, family, work, money, and every other area of life. Choices and decisions get a lot easier when you follow God's direction.

Family and friends can also share the wisdom they have based on experiences and how they've seen God work. It's important to invite wise input from a few key people who you know and trust are walking with Jesus.

Having Brains means that you "think like Jesus" and depend on the Holy Spirit.

When you pursue Jesus, two things happen – you set your mind and heart on things that matter most to God and then surrender to the Holy Spirit to lead and guide you. That means that you look to the Bible for all the answers and then pray for guidance from the Holy Spirit to apply it to your decisions. God's ways usually make hard decisions easier.

Strong Girls create a positive and powerful mindset.

You have brains that are continually being transformed by the renewing of your mind. You grow a mindset that helps you see clearly and do the right things. Mindset is everything.

Let's talk about 7 key ways to use our brains to think like Jesus and forge a positive mindset.

1. **Have an Eternal Perspective.** God tells us wisdom is found when we understand how short this life is relative to eternity. This perspective helps you choose eternal rewards over temporary satisfaction. It helps you choose what you need most over what you want now. It helps you prioritize things that will last rather than material things you will leave behind. Even though life is meant to be enjoyed, you can also prioritize long-term satisfaction over immediate gratification.

2. **Have a Clear Vision.** Creating a clear and compelling picture of what you believe God truly wants for you in life helps inspire and motivate you to keep striving for important goals. Without vision, you lack that "true north" direction that keeps you living for Christ. Vision helps you make wise decisions and reject excuses or short-cuts.

3. **Have a Growth Mindset.** Girls with brains don't worry about challenges or obstacles, instead, they see them as an opportunity to grow and learn. You see everything as an opportunity to improve and be your best. Even failure is used to become stronger and more resilient. Many people have a fixed mindset and are unwilling to take risks and tackle new challenges because they're afraid of failing. But you accept criticism because you will use it to be better. *Strong Girls* want to grow.

4. **Stay Positive & Optimistic.** There is a ton of negativity and pessimism in the world, but *Strong Girls* are positive and optimistic. You see life as a gift to be enjoyed and lived to the full. You don't take part in negativity, criticism, or complaining. You reject discouragement and defeat. You also have tremendous faith that nothing is impossible with God. He can turn around even the worst situations.

The abundance *MINDSET* is a belief in the **GOODNESS** and **GENEROSITY** of God.

5. **Replace the Lies with Truth.** Your enemy, the devil, is a liar. He wants to make you believe terrible things about yourself if he can, so you have to memorize scripture and use the truth to defeat the lies. You choose the warrior voice and not the whiny voice full of complaining and excuses. You can be certain that you belong, are loved unconditionally, and are valued.

6. **Thinks Abundance, not Scarcity.** Jesus came to give you the abundant life. The abundance mindset is a belief in the goodness and generosity of God. God has more than enough for everyone to enjoy. God's pie is limitless. Scarcity is from the enemy. It makes you think God is unfair and makes you jealous of what others have. The abundance mindset makes you dream big and see unlimited opportunities.

7. **Don't Play the Victim.** It's popular today to be a victim and use that to make excuses or blame others for why you can't do things. *Strong Girls* take responsibility and ownership for their lives and live victoriously. A victim mindset prevents you from living the abundant life.

Strong Girls have brains. You seek wisdom and apply it to every decision. And, you develop a mindset, a way of thinking, that leads to opportunity, overcoming, and a positive future.

Everyone can have brains because everyone can be wise. You are made to be wise.

KEY TRUTHS

1. Wisdom > smarts.

2. The Bible has all the answers for life.

3. Create a positive, powerful mindset.

4. Think like Jesus.

Add your own thoughts and observations:

_____

_____

_____

_____

_____

KEY VERSES

1. **Fear / Wisdom** – Proverbs 1:7
2. **Humility / Mindset** – Philippians 2:5-8
3. **Mind / Transformation** – Romans 12:2
4. **Focus / Positive** – Philippians 4:8
5. **Wisdom / Understanding** – Proverbs 4:7
6. **Focus / Mind** – Colossians 3:1-2
7. **Mind of Christ** – 1 Corinthians 2:16
8. **Ask for Wisdom** – James 1:5
9. **Trust / Direction** – Proverbs 3:5-6
10. **Time / Opportunities** – Ephesians 5:15-16
11. **Wise Friends** – Proverbs 13:20
12. **Foundation / Actions** – Matthew 7:24
13. **Life is Short** - Psalm 90:12

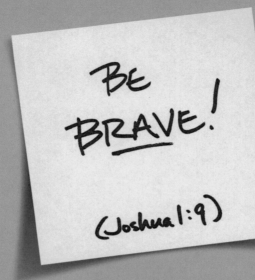

Be BRAVE!

(Joshua 1:9)

BRAWN
MADE
TO BE
BRAVE

BRAWN - MADE TO BE BRAVE

When we say *Strong Girls* have Brawn, we are referring to being **capable and courageous.** Specifically, you are physically capable and morally courageous. And that is God's design for girls.

When most of you think of "brawn", you immediately think of physical strength. And, you'd be right because that is the traditional definition and it's part of it. Taking care of your physical body is an important part of being strong. But developing the moral courage and grit plus the strength and determination to stay free and be brave regardless of the circumstances, that's true brawn.

Many girls unfortunately buy into the lie that they shouldn't be physically strong or capable. Nothing could be further from the truth. In fact, being a good steward of your physical body is super important, especially since your physical health directly affects your mental health, emotions, and even your relationships. Plus, it takes a lot of discipline and effort to be physically healthy, and those two qualities are necessary for almost every aspect of life.

***Strong Girls* are designed to be physically capable.** That means you work to have strength, endurance, and flexibility. It doesn't mean you need to be a competitive athlete, but you should be healthy and strong. Life brings lots of physical challenges and being healthy helps you handle them. Eating clean, exercising, and getting quality sleep are three big pieces of having the energy you need for life! A healthy body leads to a more positive and upbeat mindset, emotional stability, and zest for life.

***Strong Girls* are also made to be courageous.** You have the mental, emotional, spiritual, and moral courage needed to go against the cultural flow and walk in freedom in Christ. You will face pressure to violate your standards and go with the flow. You will also face an enemy that wants to keep you stuck in mistakes. You develop the resilience to bounce back from setbacks and the determination to persevere and even thrive through challenges and hardships. You have the spiritual toughness to battle against the enemy and his tactics. Brawn is the will to stay free.

Don't **SHRINK** *back.*

Part of having brawn is found in overcoming fears and trying new things. This is part of the breakthrough process that develops confidence and courage. You are designed to enjoy and experience a rich, satisfying, and meaningful life; that's what Jesus calls abundance. True brawn comes from depending on and relying on Jesus. Without brawn, you will shrink back from opportunities and miss out on this great adventure.

A *HEALTHY BODY* leads to a more *POSITIVE* and *UPBEAT* mindset, emotional stability, and *ZEST* for life.

This type of brawn comes from who you are on the inside. It's a result of the beauty (character & virtue) and brains (mindset & wisdom) you've developed; brawn puts all that into action.

Strong Girls are strong in mind, body, and spirit. They bring the brawn!

Let's talk about 7 key ways to "bring the brawn" and create true strength for an abundant life.

1. **Go For It!** Don't be afraid to try new things that you may not know about or be naturally good at. *Strong Girls* go for it. You try it even though you might not be great. This is the pathway to growth and strength. Don't let doubts or fears make you live a small life. God didn't give you a spirit of fear, but of love, power, and a sound mind.

2. **Build Spiritual Muscle!** Spiritual muscle grows when you take your personal, private relationship with Jesus and make it public. Actively live out your faith and become comfortable identifying with Jesus. Be brave enough to express your faith and live by it no matter who you are with. Don't shrink back. Put on the armor and take a stand against the schemes of the devil.

3. **Do Hard Things.** Most people will look for the easiest way. But you know that the easy way never leads to greatness. The more you seek the hard things, the more capable you become. Do hard physical work. Train outside in bad weather. Push beyond your limits. Over time, you will discover you are more capable than you think.

4. **Take Care of Your Health.** Girls are made to be physically healthy and strong. Do the necessary work. Committing to eating clean foods, exercising regularly, and sleeping better will produce positive results. Pursuing optimal physical health also makes you able to protect and defend yourself. It feels good to be fit. And it reduces anxiety and stress.

5. **Grow Resilience and Grit.** You know that life can be hard, but you also know you have what it takes to overcome challenges and obstacles. Grit is forged by doing hard things and getting outside your comfort zone. It develops a "bring it on!" mentality that makes you into an overcomer.

6. **Go Against the Flow.** Moral courage empowers you to do the right thing, no matter what. That's spiritual brawn. This requires full dependence on the power of God in you. Many friends will try to tempt you to compromise and cut corners. But you will develop the brawn to overcome those temptations and take the better path.

7. **Become Anti-fragile.** Becoming anti-fragile means you not only get through difficult times, but you use those challenges and disappointments to get stronger. You use failures as a learning experience. In fact, you look forward to and expect God to use challenges for your ultimate benefit.

Strong Girls bring the brawn. You go for it and develop a strength of body and character that makes you capable and courageous, no matter the challenge.

Everyone can have brawn because everyone can be brave. *You are made to be brave.*

KEY TRUTHS

1.   Brawn means being physically capable and morally courageous.

2.   You are more capable than you think.

3.   It's a fight to stay free.

Add your own thoughts and observations:

_____

_____

_____

_____

_____

KEY VERSES

1. **Spiritual Armor** – Ephesians 6:10-18
2. **Power not Fear** – 2 Timothy 1:7
3. **Body / Temple** – 1 Corinthians 6:19-20
4. **Strong / Courageous** – Joshua 1:9
5. **Living Sacrifice** – Romans 12:1
6. **No Fear** – Psalm 27:1
7. **Overcome Evil** – Romans 12:21
8. **Overcome Temptation** – 1 Corinthians 10:13
9. **God's Assurance** – Romans 8:31
10. **God is With You** – Psalm 23:4
11. **Be Strong** – Psalm 31:24

TRUE BRAWN

comes from

DEPENDING ON

and

RELYING ON

JESUS.

LET YOUR LIGHT SHINE!

(Mat. 5:16)

BRILIANCE
MADE TO
SHINE

BRILLIANCE - MADE TO SHINE

When we say *Strong Girls* have Brilliance, we are referring to the **freedom to shine.** And that is God's design for girls.

When most of you think of "brilliance", you may think of how a diamond captures the light and sparkles or maybe a masterful performance on stage, in the classroom, or on the athletic field.

A diamond is an impressive picture of how our life should look to others. Diamonds are like the Moon in that they don't produce light by themselves, but when light enters a diamond, it bounces around inside the many facets to produce the beautiful sparkle that we love so much. A well-cut diamond is magnificent to behold.

Strong Girls are designed to reflect and shine the light of Christ. When you get more of God's goodness inside of you, and let that goodness come out of you, other people notice. That goodness shows up in your attitude, your words, your positive energy, and how you treat others. It shows up in everything you say and do. But the really cool part is this, the brilliance others see in you points people to God and glorifies Him. (Matthew 5:14-16)

Sometimes you feel you have to be "good enough" or amazing so your light can shine. You may not feel worthy; like you're nothing special. But the truth is this – you are special because you are God's daughter. He created you. Surrender your life to be used for God's glory. You don't have to be "good enough", you just need a desire to let God's light shine through you. There is no pressure, but you will have a desire to please God in how you act.

The **BRILLIANCE** *others see in* *you* **POINTS** *people to God and* **GLORIFIES** *Him.*

Jesus sets you free. Life in Christ is not about perfection, it's about direction. Where the Spirit of the Lord is, there is freedom. Jesus came to set you free from guilt and shame so you can truly shine! When you are weighed down by sin, it's hard to shine.

But when you receive the free gift of eternal life, by grace through faith, you are set free and can live this new life! The old is gone, and the new has come.

Grace is proof of God's unconditional love for you. You can't do anything to deserve His love; He gives it to you freely. When you give God all the credit and all the glory, others are drawn to the Heavenly Father. That makes you His ambassador, and other people will be attracted to the joy and peace they see in you.

Let's talk about 7 key ways to live with the freedom to shine and reflect God's glory.

1. **Surrender Everything** – Sometimes it makes us feel better when we're in control of things. But God invites you to give Him control of your life and to trust that He loves you and has what's best for you. This isn't easy, but when you seek Him, listen to His voice, and follow in His steps, you can live with peace and confidence.

2. **Live on Purpose** – When you live with the purpose of glorifying God, your light can't help but shine. You always have a greater purpose in everything you do.

3. **Be an Ambassador** – An ambassador always represents the interests of the one they serve. That means that you bring His truth and principles everywhere you go.

4. **Do Good Deeds** – God created you to do good works to bless others. There are always little and big things you can do to make someone's day.

5. **Bear Fruit** – Fruit is the evidence of a life being lived for God. It can be inside fruit like character and virtue or outside fruit like people trusting in Jesus. You cultivate the soil; God is responsible for producing the fruit.

6. **Turn Trials into Testimonies** – Sometimes you shine the brightest by the way you handle hard times. God's presence is often brightest when the circumstances are darkest. You will shine brightest when you are at your weakest, because God shows up at His strongest.

7. **Make a Difference** – Your light shines bright when you are unselfish and truly want to be a positive force in the world. This life is not about you; it's about building God's Kingdom.

Strong Girls shine! You live with grace and freedom, not weighed down by mistakes of the past or anxious about the future.

Everyone can have brilliance because everyone can be free. You are made to shine.

GOD's
PRESENCE
is often
BRIGHTEST
when the
circumstances are
DARKEST.

KEY TRUTHS

1. Jesus sets you free.

2. When you surrender, you win.

3. It's all about Jesus.

Add your own thoughts and observations:

_____

_____

_____

_____

_____

KEY VERSES

1. **He Lives in You** – Galatians 2:20
2. **Saved by Grace** – Ephesians 2:8-9
3. **Do Good** – Titus 2:7-8
4. **Set the Example** – 1 Timothy 4:12
5. **Shine your light** – Matthew 5:14-16
6. **Rejoice / Pray / Give Thanks** – 1 Thessalonians 5:16-18
7. **Whatever You Do** – Colossians 3:17
8. **Christ's Ambassadors** – 2 Corinthians 5:20
9. **You are Free** – 2 Corinthians 3:17
10. **The New is Here** – 2 Corinthians 5:17
11. **Bear Fruit** – Galatians 5:22-23
12. **Stay Connected** – John 15:5
13. **Good Works** – Ephesians 2:10
14. **Live in the Light** – Ephesians 5:8

37
EXERCISES

STRENGTH
TRAINING

The next

37 EXERCISES

will forge you into a strong girl

with unstoppable

CHARACTER, CONFIDENCE, AND COURAGE.

You will find 'sticky principles'

tied to unchanging truths

in God's Word that will

mold you into the person

you're made to be.

REMEMBER...

The see it, stop it, start it formula for growth is the "secret sauce" of *Strong Girls*. It's a simple and powerful way to examine your life, decide, and take action to stop destructive behavior and start consistent behaviors that lead to life.

1. **SEE IT** – be honest as you look for areas of your life that need to get better and "see it".

2. **STOP IT** – commit to one thing you can stop doing that is preventing you from improving.

3. **START IT** – commit to one thing to start doing consistently that will help you be your best.

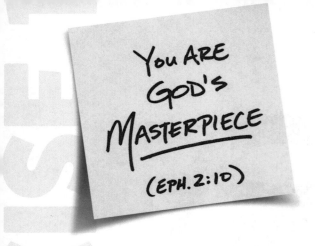

YOU ARE GOD'S MASTERPIECE

(EPH. 2:10)

For we are God's masterpiece, created in Christ Jesus to do good works, which God prepared in advance for us to do.

– Ephesians 2:10

GRACE'S STORY

"I've had a hard time thinking of myself as a masterpiece. Especially when I've made mistakes or decisions that I knew weren't right. It's been hard to believe that God sees His finished work in my life and that He's pleased even when my life is a bit of a mess. Knowing that God is making me into a beautiful person motivates me to trust Him and become everything I'm made to be. It also makes me want to be my best."

GET STRONG

A masterpiece refers to someone's greatest work created with masterful skill. You usually think of a painting or sculpture like the Mona Lisa, the Statue of David, or even the Statue of Liberty. But, it could also be a movie, a book, a speech, or even a performance crafted with extraordinary talent and love.

You are God's Masterpiece. You are the work of art. And the one who created the universe – the heavens and the earth and everything in them – is the one putting you together as a master craftsman. He sees who you are right now and who you will be when the masterpiece is complete. God is the ultimate artist. And He is creating you with a unique design in mind, so there is no one else quite like you. You are not an accident.

Before you took your first breath, God had a vision of who you would become. He saw your personality's intricate details and your unique talents and strengths. God saw the mistakes you would make, your triumphs, and your journey of growth.

He sees the beauty of His creation even when it looks messy or unfinished. You will have days when you don't feel very special or you don't like things about yourself. And that's ok.

Adolescence is a period of ups and downs. It's full of inconsistency in making choices.

You are still His masterpiece, even when you don't feel like it. Even when you make a mistake, did something you wish you didn't, or said something you wish you could take back. He sees the finished work, the masterpiece you are, and who you're destined to be.

In those moments when you doubt your worth or feel imperfect, remember that God sees you as His masterpiece and His work is not done yet!

THINGS I WOULD TELL MY YOUNGER SELF

"How you feel about yourself doesn't change how God feels about you. And nothing you can do will ever make Him stop crafting you into a masterpiece. Don't expect to be perfect because no one is. Give yourself a break and know that in God's eyes, you are one-of-a-kind."

SEE IT — STOP IT — START IT

1. What does it mean to be God's Masterpiece?

2. When do you feel like less than a masterpiece?

3. What happens when you live like you're a mess, not a masterpiece?

What do you **SEE?** _____

_____

What are you going to **STOP?**_____

_____

What are you going to **START?** _____

_____

Key Verses: Psalm 139:13-14, Isaiah 64:8, 1 Peter 2:9, Jeremiah 29:11, Philippians 1:6

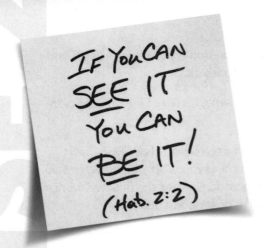

If You CAN
SEE IT
You CAN
BE IT!
(Hab. 2:2)

Then the LORD answered me and said, 'Write down the vision and inscribe it clearly on tablets, so that one who reads it may run.'

– Habakkuk 2:2

GRACE'S STORY

"Me, my Dad, my brother John, and friend Gabi were on our way to Wyoming to go snowmobiling when we encountered an incredible blizzard. We kept driving as conditions got worse. We were 15 minutes away from the place when we could no longer see the road ahead. It was a complete white-out. Even though my Dad's Jeep could handle the snow, we couldn't continue without vision. We never reached our destination."

GET STRONG

Life without vision is full of detours and dead ends. But life with vision is a great adventure!

Every elite athlete, musician, or performer has a clear vision of what an optimal performance looks like. In fact, they 'visualize' the performance in detail before they even take the field or stage. They know if they can see it, they can achieve it. That's why you need a clear vision of what an amazing life looks like.

Vision is a clear picture of a desired future reality. True vision for life comes from God; the one who created you has plans to make you into a masterpiece. When you seek God, He gives you that vision. Then He gives you the wisdom and His Word to light your path along the way. Without it, you will be confused and make poor decisions.

Vision is a powerful tool that gives you a target to shoot for. It provides intention and direction, and inspires you to action. Vision reveals the difference between who you are now and who you can be, motivating you to close that gap. However, if self-interest motivates you, you will end up feeling unfulfilled and empty.

In Habakkuk 2:2, you learn that vision must be so simple and clear that "a herald may run with it". It's so short and clear you can carry it, memorize it, and easily pass it on.

When it's simple, clear, and meaningful, it motivates you to go after it. And it inspires others to help you and rallies them behind you to fulfill the vision.

You need a vision for your health, your relationships, school, and even your work. There are many ways to capture your vision – a vision board with pictures of what's most important to you is an easy way to get started. If you can see it, you can be it.

THINGS I WOULD TELL MY YOUNGER SELF

*"**Create a super clear picture of how you see the future.** Ask God to reveal His plans for you, your health, your relationships, and your mission. Then make a vision board and keep it front and center."*

SEE IT — STOP IT — START IT

1   Why is vision for your future so important?

2.   What do you want most for your life, and why is it important?

3.   Seek God and describe who you will become.

What do you **SEE?** _____

_____

What are you going to **STOP?** _____

_____

What are you going to **START?** _____

_____

Key Verses: Proverbs 29:18, Isaiah 30:21, Jeremiah 29:11, Acts 2:17, Hebrew 11:1

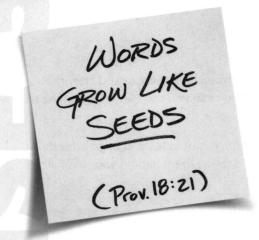

WORDS
GROW LIKE
SEEDS

(Prov. 18:21)

The tongue has the power of life and death, and those who love it will eat its fruit.

– Proverbs 18:21

GRACE'S STORY

"For me, the words that I thought and spoke about myself and to myself were often the harshest. But I also let things that others said, even "friends," affect me negatively. So much so that it got me down and I believed their criticism. The fruit of that negativity was that I believed the lies. It caused a lack of confidence in myself that led to compromise, and I eventually had to get new friends."

GET STRONG

When you plant seeds in the ground, with a little water and sunshine, it doesn't take long before you see a little seedling sprouting out of the soil. Soon after it will produce whatever you planted – a fruit or vegetable or maybe even a flower.

Your words grow like seeds. When you speak a word, it gets planted in your mind and grows. And in the end, it will bear fruit just like a seed in the ground.

Everything you say has the power to bring life or death, not just for you, but also for others. The words you plant can be positive or negative, encouraging or discouraging. They can lift others up or tear them down. They can be challenging or critical, helpful or hurtful. Even a casual or careless word or something said as a joke can grow over time into something very destructive and cause lasting pain. Words that bless and build can even change your direction and destiny. Once you say words, it is impossible to take them back. That makes the things you say super important.

You plant words like seeds with what you say to yourself and others. And when you say those things often enough, it's like you are planting an entire garden of positive or negative words. You will eventually "eat [the] fruit" and it will either make you healthy or sick. Words like "I'm not good enough, pretty enough, or smart enough" will produce a garden of negativity. Words like "I can, I'm strong, or it's possible" will produce a garden of positivity and faith.

Be careful and intentional with the words you plant so they bear good fruit. Most of us take things that are said personally and they stick with us for a long time. So make sure that the words you speak to yourself and others bring life.

THINGS I WOULD TELL MY YOUNGER SELF

"Cut off the negative immediately. Don't let words that make you feel bad about yourself grow. Stay positive. And don't believe the lies. Surround yourself with positive people who lift you up with their words. If someone constantly tears you down, they're definitely not your friend."

SEE IT — STOP IT — START IT

1. What negative words have you said about yourself? Others?

2. What negative, hurtful, or critical words have others said to you that you still remember?

3. Who might need you to bless them with uplifting words this week?

What do you **SEE?** _____

_____

What are you going to **STOP?** _____

_____

What are you going to **START?** _____

_____

Key Verses: Proverbs 15:4, James 3:5-6, Ephesians 4:29

TAKE
JESUS
EVERYWHERE

(Luke 9:23)

*Whoever wants to be
my disciple must deny
themselves and take
up their cross daily and
follow me.*

– Luke 9:23

GRACE'S STORY

*"I was two different people depending on who I was with. At church, I
was the 'church girl.' At school, it wasn't popular to be a Christian or do
things differently from everybody else, so I acted differently. I was lying
and hiding. I would wear one thing to school that my parents approved
of, then change when I got there. I would check Jesus at the door. After a
while, this created stress and wore me out."*

GET STRONG

It's easy to make your relationship with Jesus "one part" of your life.
You've got lots of pieces in your life like school, work, family, friends,
activities, social media, church, and many more. So it's kind of easy to put
Jesus in the church or devotional "box" and then not really bring Him into
the other areas of your life.

God designed us to take Jesus everywhere. It's easy to identify with Jesus
at church, but it may not be so easy when you're with your friends or in a
relationship. He's not part of your life; He is your life. He's not something;
he's everything.

When Jesus said that to be his disciple, you have to deny yourself, pick
up your cross, and follow Him, He emphasized you would take Him into
every area of your life. The reason this is so important is because you
don't want to act like two different people depending on who you're with
or where you go.

You don't want to leave Jesus outside when you go to the party; you take
Him with you. You don't want to take Him with you with your church

friends, but leave Him behind with your other friends. You don't want to post something on social media that would be inappropriate with Jesus right there with you.

When you take Jesus everywhere, you become a person of character and integrity. You become the same person regardless of who you're with, where you go, or what you do. And it feels good to live like that. It's hard to be two different people.

Jesus is always with you, even when you think you're leaving Him behind. When you are a follower of Jesus, His Spirit lives in you and never leaves. Live that truth and take Jesus everywhere.

THINGS I WOULD TELL MY YOUNGER SELF

"If you love Jesus, act like it all the time. Don't leave Jesus behind and pretend to be someone you're not just to fit in; it wears you out."

SEE IT — STOP IT — START IT

1. Are you the same person no matter who you are with, where you go, or what you do?

2. In what ways do you "leave Jesus behind"?

3. What will you commit to do to take Jesus with you everywhere? What may need to change?

What do you **SEE?** _____

_____

What are you going to **STOP?** _____

_____

What are you going to **START?** _____

_____

Key Verses: Philippians 1:21, Galatians 2:20, Matthew 10:38-39

GRACE'S STORY

*"My parents wouldn't let me quit something once I committed to it.
Whether it was in sports or school, I had to finish. If I wasn't getting
playing time, or was struggling, sometimes I got discouraged. I learned
that the only failure is when you give up. Setbacks along the way
are normal; but refusing to quit and persevering to the end built the
confidence and courage I need for life."*

GET STRONG

When Bethany Hamilton was just 13 years old, a shark off the coast of
Hawaii attacked her and she suffered the loss of her left arm. It was a
tragic event that nearly cost her life. Incredibly, she returned to surfing
just one month after the attack and became one of the top professional
surfers in the world.

It would have been easy to quit under those circumstances. Most people
didn't even think it was possible to surf with just one arm. But she was
passionate and determined to find a way. That spirit empowered her to
overcome incredible disappointment, all the doubts in her head, and all
the critics and naysayers.

You've probably heard, "when the going gets tough, the tough get
going." It's a great reminder that there will be tough times, but if you have
the right character, you will keep going. Perseverance, resilience, and
refusing to quit are key components of a strong and virtuous character.
Challenging times create opportunities for God to refine your character
and develop strength and compassion and faith through trials. That

process takes time and is hard, but it's worth it.

If Bethany would have given up after her tragic accident, we never would have heard her story and millions would have missed out on her example and encouragement to never give up.

As a believer in Jesus, you're made to do good things. You're made to bring your faith everywhere and share it often. God refers to that as planting seeds. Sometimes that can be a challenge and can discourage because you may not see a positive impact immediately. But God promises you will reap a harvest if you persevere, if you don't give up.

You are responsible for planting; He handles the growth. Never give up.

THINGS I WOULD TELL MY YOUNGER SELF

"If you are confident you are doing what God wants, do it all out. Don't give up when things get hard or you experience discouragement. When you persevere, God will not only see you through the tough spots, He will impact others, too."

SEE IT — STOP IT — START IT

1. What challenges have you faced where you wanted to give up?

2. What helped you to persevere and stick it out?

3. In what ways did your character grow in strength through that process?

What do you **SEE?** _____

_____

What are you going to **STOP?** _____

_____

What are you going to **START?** _____

_____

Key Verses: 1 Corinthians 15:58, Hebrews 12:1-2, 2 Corinthians 4:16-18

Do
HARD
THINGS
(2 Cor. 6:4)

Rather, as servants of God we commend ourselves in every way; in great endurance; in troubles, hardships and distresses...

– 2 Corinthians 6:4

GRACE'S STORY

"My Dad was after me for the longest time to do a mental toughness program called 75Hard. I didn't want to do it and made up every excuse I could think of to avoid it. He said if I finished the 75 days in a row without failing, it would transform the way I approach every challenge. Well, he was right. My mindset now is this – I do hard things."

GET STRONG

Life is good, but it can be hard too. That's not a bad thing, but it's good to know so you are prepared for the hard things. The key is to discover that you are capable of handling hard things.

Paul knew discomfort and hardship very well. In fact, he didn't see it as something to be avoided. He saw it as a way to become everything he was made to be. He never shied away from doing hard things, and it strengthened his determination to persevere.

Resilience is one of the most important qualities you can develop to weather the storms of life. It's the ability to go through a lot of really hard stuff and bounce back better. It's a mix of grit and toughness and confidence wrapped into one. You can't develop any of these qualities unless you will do hard things.

We chose to do the 75Hard mental toughness program to push us outside our comfort zones and develop discipline and grit. For 75 consecutive days, we did 2 workouts, followed a nutrition plan, drank a gallon of water, and read 10 pages. The program challenged us physically, mentally, and emotionally. It pushed both of us to face our excuses and stop taking shortcuts. There is something very empowering when you willingly do hard things; it forges character and confidence.

We're wired to seek comfort, take the easy path, and avoid pain. But to become resilient, you need a mindset that enjoys discomfort. That mindset helps you become the type of person who looks forward to hard things. You see adversity not as something to be avoided, but as an opportunity to grow and get better. You get comfortable being uncomfortable. As you take on greater challenges, you get stronger and able to overcome even bigger obstacles.

To be your best, do hard things. Take on the "I do hard things" mindset and identity.

THINGS I WOULD TELL MY YOUNGER SELF

"See every challenge as an opportunity to prove what you are capable of doing. When facing something hard, don't hesitate; go for it. The struggle is what will ultimately grow your confidence."

SEE IT — STOP IT — START IT

1.   Do you typically avoid hard things or look forward to them?

2.   What are some 'hard things' you can choose to do to get better?

3.   How might tackling hard things help you grow physically, mentally, and spiritually?

What do you **SEE?** _____

_____

What are you going to **STOP?** _____

_____

What are you going to **START?** _____

_____

Key Verses: Romans 5:3-4, 2 Timothy 2:3, Romans 8:18

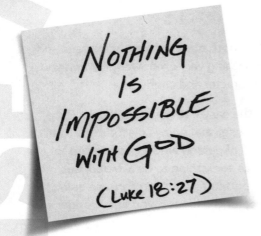

What is impossible with man is possible with God.

– Luke 18:27

GRACE'S STORY

"I transferred to an all-girls Catholic school for my freshman year of high school. I tried out for the varsity swim team, even though I'd never swum competitively in my life. When I told my Dad I had only two weeks to get ready, he said 'we better get to work!' As an athlete, I thought it'd be easy, but I learned quickly that water is very different from land! We trusted God would close the gap fast, put in the work, and I made the team, proving to me that nothing is impossible with God."

GET STRONG

The Navy SEALS say when you feel like quitting, you're only 40% of the way there. That means that if you just did 4 pushups and think you couldn't possibly do one more, you can actually do 6 more reps! What you think is impossible is just hard. You have much more inside you; you just need to believe it.

They call that the 40% Rule and use it to get the very best out of everyone trying to be a SEAL. They redefine what you believe is possible.

Whatever you're facing may seem impossible to face or fix. Like you've done everything you could and just want to quit or give up. But remember, you have the power of the Holy Spirit living in you; the same power that created the heavens and earth and raised Jesus from the dead. That source of power turns what seems impossible into possible. It turns your 40% into 100%.

There are so many challenges in life that will make you want to give up. That's why this truth that 'nothing is impossible with God' is so important.

It doesn't mean everything will go your way, but it will help you dig in and discover you have much more inside yourself.

Maybe things are hard at home, or maybe you are tackling an enormous challenge. You don't think you have anything left in the tank; you don't think you can do it. And just moments before a breakthrough, you are tempted to give up and you'll never know what might have been.

That's the exact moment you need to trust God and believe you have it in you. You can do more physically. You can handle more challenges. Next time, instead of giving up, rely on Jesus to get you through and help you get that last 60%.

THINGS I WOULD TELL MY YOUNGER SELF

"When you feel like quitting, you're only 40% of the way there. Ask God to give you the strength you need to keep going and overcome! Otherwise, you might miss the blessing of success."

SEE IT — STOP IT — START IT

1. What challenge seems impossible for you right now?

2. In what ways might God be able to turn it around?

3. What can you do to persevere and stick it out as you rely on God?

What do you **SEE?** _____

_____

What are you going to **STOP?** _____

_____

What are you going to **START?** _____

_____

Key Verses: Romans 8:11, Luke 1:37, Mark 10:27

We demolish arguments and every pretension that sets itself up against the knowledge of God, and we take captive every thought to make it obedient to Christ.

– 2 Corinthians 10:5

GRACE'S STORY

"I have to admit, after elementary school, I never really liked school very much. Mostly because I didn't think I was smart. I remember saying, 'I'm no good at school' and 'I'm just not smart' all the time and it hurt my grades. My parents quickly confronted those words and asked, 'Is that truth or trash?' Because I thought it and said it out loud, I came to believe it. When I had success in college classes I enjoyed, I realized you can't believe everything you think."

GET STRONG

Not every thought that you think is true; and not every thought is good for you, either. In fact, we have an enemy whose name is liar and deceiver. He plants thoughts that are deceptive and destructive. His desire is to separate us from God by sowing seeds (thoughts) of doubt that lead to disobedience.

That's why it's so important that you don't believe everything you think. You must question if that is a thought from God, the enemy, or even just your own weakness. Sometimes thoughts pop into our head from things someone said a long time ago. Sometimes we say things and the enemy uses those words against us to control our feelings.

No matter where the thought comes from, you must control them, or they will control you. You must confront and dismantle negative or destructive thoughts that don't align with the truth of God. If you believe every thought you have, you will get discouraged. This is not a one-time battle; it's an every-day, all-the-time fight we must win.

We used to play a game called "truth or trash"; every time someone would say something negative like "I'm not smart" or "I can't do it" or "I'm going to fail" or "Nobody likes me", we would challenge it and ask – "Is that truth or trash?" We would then test it against the truth of God's word. If it was something God would agree with, then it was the truth. But often, those words were trash.

If you start to believe the trash, it will eventually become poisonous to you and prevent you from becoming everything God made you to be. You must take out the trash and replace the trash with the truth like – "Nothing is impossible with God" or "When I am weak, God is strong" or "I can do all things through Christ who strengthens me."

Don't believe everything you think.

THINGS I WOULD TELL MY YOUNGER SELF

"Confront every thought and determine if it's truth or trash. You can't let lies stick around in your head because, before long, you will believe them. Take out the trash and refuse to believe the lies."

SEE IT – STOP IT – START IT

1. What lies (trash) are you believing that are hurting you?

2. What truth can you replace that trash with?

What do you **SEE?** _____

_____

What are you going to **STOP?** _____

_____

What are you going to **START?** _____

_____

Key Verses: Romans 12:1-2, Philippians 4:8

KEEP YOUR
INNER CIRCLE
SMALL

(Prov. 18:24)

A [person] of many companions may come to ruin, but there is a friend who sticks closer than a brother.

– Proverbs 18:24

GRACE'S STORY

"I had a hard time knowing who my genuine friends were. I wanted to be liked, and it felt good to have a big friend group. I shared important things with lots of friends, and it backfired. Some who I trusted turned their backs on me when I needed them most. I quickly found myself on the outside of the group. It takes time to know who you can trust and to discern who shares your faith and values; those you can depend on in good times and bad."

GET STRONG

Everyone likes to be liked. We like to have friends. Some people like to have a lot of friends and others are happy with just a few good friends.

Jesus had thousands of followers in real life. They followed Him around listening to His teaching and being healed and set free. Stories of feeding the 5,000 were regular occurrences. Crowds formed around Him like mobs just to touch His robe and be healed.

Today, you would say that Jesus had a lot of friends and followers; He was an influencer. If He had a podcast, it would be #1 by a mile.

But in truth, He had very few very close friends. He traveled exclusively with 12 men who He invested nearly all His time with. Jesus hung out with this small group and gave the 12 disciples inside information. They shared meals and games; they cried, prayed, celebrated, and laughed together.

Even within the 12 though, Jesus had a very close, tight-knit group of three best friends – Peter, James and John. He knew the power and importance of a small inner circle of friends. Jesus trusted them completely.

These three were "friends who stick closer than a brother." These three witnessed His agony in the garden before His betrayal. They witnessed miraculous healings. And He trusted them to build His church after His resurrection.

You need to be like Jesus. Keep your inner circle small. You may have a group of friends you do lots of things with. But don't share everything about you and your life with everybody; they truly can't be trusted at that level. Reserve important things for your inner circle of highly trusted friends.

THINGS I WOULD TELL MY YOUNGER SELF

"Not everybody can be a close, trusted friend. Developing trust takes time, so you shouldn't share everything with everyone. Gradually share important things with a friend or two and test whether they keep your trust. You will discover who you can really count on."

SEE IT — STOP IT — START IT

1. Do you have an inner circle of very close friends who you trust?

2. Have you had someone you thought was a friend end up gossiping or turning their back on you?

3. What qualities do you look for in an "inner circle" friend?

What do you **SEE?** _____

_____

What are you going to **STOP?** _____

_____

What are you going to **START?** _____

_____

Key Verses: Mark 9:2-8, Mark 14:32-42, Mark 5:37-43

KEEP YOUR
HEAD, UP!
^ AND HEART
(Col. 3:1-2)

Since, then, you have been raised with Christ, set your hearts on things above, where Christ is, seated at the right hand of God. Set your minds on things above, not on earthly things.

– Colossians 3:1-2

GRACE'S STORY

"My first year playing lacrosse in Colorado was a challenge. The expectations were high since I played an 'east coast' style of play against the best competition. Lacrosse was a big part of my identity. It turned out my physical style led to yellow cards, conflict with my coach, and reduced playing time. I got discouraged. The more I focused on my problems, the more frustrated I felt. It wasn't until I picked my head up, got my focus off my disappointment, and placed it on the goodness of God that my attitude changed and lacrosse got fun again."

GET STRONG

It's easy to be discouraged. When you focus on your circumstances, challenges, and everything that's not going your way, your head drops and heart sinks. When you keep your head down and focused on your problems, your heart feels heavy.

But when you keep your head up and focus on God's purpose, God lightens and lifts your heart as well. When you keep your head up, you see from an entirely different perspective. Things aren't as bad as they seem. Then you realize you're not alone and everyone has their own struggles, too. But best of all, you realize you have a lot to be thankful for.

When you keep your head up, you become more positive and optimistic. You witness all the good things you've been blessed with, like family, friends, and good health. You realize God is way bigger than your problems, giving you a sense of confidence and peace. When you focus on things that matter most to God, He changes what's most important to you. Looking to the heavens even helps you breathe more deeply and puts a smile on your face!

The simple statement to keep your head up reminds you to trust that God is in control and to not take things so seriously. It also gives you an opportunity to ask God for help instead of trying to do everything on your own.

When you make a mistake, keep your head up. When you fail to live up to your standard, keep your head up. When you feel alone or discouraged, you guessed it, keep your head up.

THINGS I WOULD TELL MY YOUNGER SELF

"Stay focused on the goodness of God and things you're thankful for. Challenges come and go. Disappointments will turn around. But you can take an active role in keeping your head and heart up. Don't wallow in your problems. Keep your head up."

SEE IT — STOP IT — START IT

1. Do you mostly have your head down focused on your challenges, or your head up focused on God's power and purpose?

2. What distracts and weighs you down most?

3. How can 'keeping your head up' lift your heart as well?

What do you **SEE?** _____

_____

What are you going to **STOP?** _____

_____

What are you going to **START?** _____

_____

Key Verses: Proverbs 4:23, Isaiah 26:3, 1 Peter 5:7

> *A generous person will prosper; whoever refreshes others will be refreshed.*
>
> – Proverbs 11:25

GRACE'S STORY

"It's impossible to be focused on yourself and others at the same time. When you focus on making a positive impact on others, it gets your eyes off yourself. For me, it was hardest to focus on helping others when I was worried about myself. I toggled between being selfish and unselfish, depending on how I felt. I didn't like the 'mood swings' and discovered that it's hard to be down when I'm looking for ways to pick others up; helping others improved my attitude."

GET STRONG

Chick-fil-a has a reputation for closing on Sundays, offering a spicy chicken sandwich, and using the phrase "my pleasure." But what they want to be known for is finding creative ways to love their customers. They go out of their way to help people in ways that have nothing to do with serving food.

They live the "make their day" philosophy. You may have heard the stories of an employee getting a cell phone a customer dropped by climbing down into a sewer drain. Another changed the tire for a WWII veteran in the parking lot. These are incredible acts of kindness and there are many more just like it!

When you "make their day" you are encouraging, building up, and refreshing others. You are actively on-the-lookout for ways to love and meet their needs. The heart of "make their day" is a genuine care for others and desire to help. You see a need and meet it.

When someone does this today, it's often so unexpected that it surprises ple. It restores people's faith and inspires them to do the same for someone else. That is exactly how acts of kindness work – they spread. Refreshing others is an act of generosity. And the benefit you get is better than what you give. God rewards those who bless others.

There are many ways to encourage, care for, help, build up, comfort, and serve others to make their day. It can be as simple as listening with full attention, writing a post-it note, running an errand, or remembering a birthday. Maybe it's a small, unexpected gift, praising someone in public, or praying for someone who's sad.

This is a practical way to model what it looks like to follow Jesus by refreshing others. In the end, you too will be refreshed. Make their day!

THINGS I WOULD TELL MY YOUNGER SELF

"Whenever you are down or discouraged, make someone else's day. The fastest way to get out of a funk is to encourage someone else. God always lifts your spirits when you lift others. Keep your eyes open for opportunities to bless."

SEE IT — STOP IT — START IT

1.   Why is it important to look for ways to serve others and make their day?

2.   Why does blessing others in a tangible way refresh yourself?

3.   Who are three people that need you to make their day? How will you do it?

What do you **SEE?** _____

_____

What are you going to **STOP?** _____

_____

What are you going to **START?** _____

_____

Key Verses: 1 Thessalonians 5:11, Romans 12:10, Philippians 2:3-4

God's WAY
Is A
BLESSING
NoT A
BURDEN.
(1 John 5:3)

In fact, this is love for God: to keep his commands. And his commands are not burdensome.

- 1 John 5:3

GRACE'S STORY

"I had a stretch of time when I really didn't like being told what I had to do. Especially if I was being told to clean up my room. But then I would get frustrated when I found my clean clothes mixed up in my 'dirty clothes' pile! It turned out that my parents told me to do certain things for my benefit. My parents always designed the tasks and rules to protect my wellbeing and for my good. I discovered God does the same thing."

GET STRONG

Sometimes people say that having a relationship with Jesus and trying to be a Christian is hard. They may even say it's heavy trying to do the right things or stand up for what they believe when so many people don't. But that's not the way God designed your life as a Christian.

You don't have to try to be a Christian. You are a Christian the moment you turn away from your sin, turn toward Jesus, believe in Him and receive the free gift of eternal life. That makes you His child, and you are a new creation.

Jesus said that He came to set us free from the burdens of trying to be perfect or good enough. He came to set you free from the weight of guilt and shame for the mistakes you've made. He doesn't want you weighed down by the past, anxious about today, or worried about the future.

In fact, He came to give you abundant life. The way you experience that full, joyful life and show your love for God is by doing what He tells you to do. And, according to the verse above, His commands are not heavy. They aren't a burden; they lead to life. Some things like 'loving your enemies' or

EXERCISE 12

'blessing those who curse you' are hard, but they are still the right thing to do.

He never asks us to try to earn His favor by being good enough. Instead, He encourages you to be joyful as you strive to keep His commands and live for Him. He knows you won't be perfect; He just wants you to make progress.

God's ways are always best. His commands, even the ones that seem to restrict you from doing things that others can do, are designed for your blessing and benefit. Boundaries lead to freedom and life. So remember, God's way is a blessing, not a burden.

THINGS I WOULD TELL MY YOUNGER SELF

"God's way is always best. Keeping God's commands is a way of expressing how much you love and trust Him. If you choose God's way, you will be blessed.

SEE IT – STOP IT – START IT

1. In what ways does living for God seem heavy or hard?

2. What is the difference between effort and earning?

3. How do God's commands and boundaries protect you and lead to life?

What do you **SEE?** _____

_____

What are you going to **STOP?** _____

_____

What are you going to **START?** _____

_____

Key Verses: John 10:10, Galatians 5:1, John 8:32

SET
THE
STANDARD

(Col. 1:10)

...live a life worthy of the Lord and please Him in every way: bearing fruit in every good work, growing in the knowledge of God, being strengthened with all power...

– Colossians 1:10

GRACE'S STORY

"As an athlete, I know what it means to live up to a standard. A standard is a commitment to a set of beliefs, expectations, and behaviors. It puts what you stand for in writing so you can hold yourself accountable to doing what you say. I faced many opportunities to cut corners, take shortcuts, and compromise. Sometimes I stood strong while other times I fell short. The best thing I did was share it with my inner circle so they could hold me accountable."

GET STRONG

Everyone who has achieved greatness has created a list of standards that they committed to live by. Creating a standard creates targets to shoot for that inspire you to be your best and please God.

Your Standard reminds you of what's most important to you. It helps you make good, moral decisions when tempted to do things that don't match up with your values.

The easiest way to set your standard is to think about what kind of person you want to be. The verse above encourages you to live in such a way that pleases the Lord; that it makes Him happy. It also encourages you to live with purpose. Three simple areas that you can set the standard for your behavior are mind, body, and spirit.

Mind: *I Stay Positive* – I win the battle of the mind, crushing the lies of the enemy that attempt to discourage by focusing on what is true and right.

Body: **I Stay Pure** – I honor God by pursuing excellent health, dressing modestly, and protecting myself from sexual sin.

Spirit: **I Stay Connected** – I spend time in God's Word, listen to worship music, and connect with other people who are pursuing Jesus.

Every statement needs to be easy to remember, meaningful to you, and something you're committed to. Remember, setting your standard will help you become who you're made to be. By setting your standard and living by it, you will attract others with high standards, too. Others around you will want to be their best. You will make mistakes and fall short; no worries. Just shake that off and get back on track. Set the Standard.

THINGS I WOULD TELL MY YOUNGER SELF

"Set a high standard for who you want to be and how you will do life. It's a key part of living a life that pleases God. Don't compromise to fit in when others do it differently. If you aim high, even if you fall short, you're going to succeed."

SEE IT – STOP IT – START IT

1. What are your standards that you will strive to live up to?

2. What are some things you will do / not do, as you seek to live a life worthy of the Lord?

3. How will your standard help you with school, work, relationships, your health, and life?

What do you **SEE?** _____

_____

What are you going to **STOP?** _____

_____

What are you going to **START?** _____

_____

Key Verses: 1 Timothy 4:12, Philippians 1:27, 1 Peter 1:15-16

Then Caleb silenced the [complaining] people before Moses and said, "We should go up and take possession of the land, for we can certainly do it.

– Numbers 13:30

GRACE'S STORY

"For a long time, my attitude was based on circumstances. If things were going good, I had a good attitude. But if they weren't, I was negative. I let my feelings determine my attitude. So, if I felt left out by friends, was struggling on the lacrosse field, or had conflict at home, I had a bad attitude. It wasn't until I decided to choose my attitude, regardless of how I felt, that I could stay positive. I counted my blessings and got better sleep, and that helped a lot, too."

GET STRONG

Attitude is everything. In fact, your attitude affects your energy, effort, expectations, and the results you get. If you have a positive attitude, it fills you with energy and helps you overcome even the toughest challenges. If you have a negative attitude, everything seems worse than it is.

Our attitudes are contagious, for better or worse. If one person is complaining or negative, it's easy to fall into the trap and become negative. No one likes to be around negative people. A positive person can turn all that around and make people more optimistic and hopeful.

Joshua and Caleb were the original "can-do" kids! They stayed positive even in the face of a big obstacle. God had just set the Israelites free from 400 years of slavery and hardship in Egypt. Right before they were to enter the Promised Land, Moses sent out 12 spies to scout out the land. Ten came back with a negative, fearful, "we can't do it" report. The "positive 2" gave a positive, faith-filled, "we can do it" report because they focused on God's power and promises. The challenge was big, but God was bigger.

Joshua and Caleb were the two that made it to the Promised Land.

We can feed the positive in these simple ways:

1. Focus on the good things you are thankful for.

2. Surround yourself with positive people.

3. Remind yourself of the promises and power of God.

We can't always choose the challenges or hard things we face. But we can choose our attitude. Life will have a bunch of ups and downs. Sometimes things will go your way; other times, they won't. Stay Positive.

THINGS I WOULD TELL MY YOUNGER SELF

"Stay Positive, even when you don't feel like it. It's not a good idea to be led around by your feelings because your feelings change so fast. Instead, focus on how good God is and what you're thankful for, and then your feelings will follow your attitude."

SEE IT — STOP IT — START IT

1. When facing a really big challenge or disappointment, are you usually positive or negative?

2. What are the things you are most positive about? Most negative about?

3. What are some things you can do to choose your attitude and be more positive?

What do you **SEE?** _____

_____

What are you going to **STOP?** _____

_____

What are you going to **START?** _____

_____

Key Verses: Philippians 4:8, 2 Corinthians 10:5

STAY TIGHT
TO
JESUS

(MAT. 11:29)

*Take my yoke upon you
and learn from me, for I
am gentle and humble in
heart, and you will find
rest for your souls.*

- Matthew 11:29

GRACE'S STORY

*"I always wanted to have a best friend who I knew I could count on.
Most of the time, we were all part of a group. I had good friends, like in
school and on my teams, but having that one 'best friend' was always
a challenge. You know, that person you do everything with. I eventually
realized Jesus wanted to be that friend for me. Walking with Jesus gave
me a sense of security. And when that happened, I put less pressure on
my friendships and became a better friend, too."*

GET STRONG

Walk with Jesus. Sounds easy enough, right? And that's exactly what
Jesus wants you to do. He wants to be your best friend – the one you
count on and confide in.

A yoke is a wooden beam used to harness two animals together for
work. This works for horses and oxen because it brings two powerful
animals together to plow a field or pull a load. It makes them powerful and
productive.

Jesus invites you to take His yoke upon you in the same way. It connects
you to Him so you can learn from His example and work together to do
good things. He is a friend and understands exactly how you feel and
what you need. Nobody loves you or wants better for you than Jesus.

He promises that when you walk with him, you will find rest and peace.
It seems odd because a yoke almost always shows there will be work.
That's the beauty of walking with Jesus; He makes even hard work have
purpose.

Walking with Jesus is just like having a best friend, only better. He is the best listener, and He understands everything you will ever go through. He also gives you wise advice for anything you are facing. Plus, He's never too busy or unavailable.

When you walk with Jesus, you surrender control and direction to Him. You let Him teach you and guide you. You listen to His wisdom, watch how He acts and treats people, and walk in his ways. You won't be able to go off on your own and destroy the field. When you surrender to His lead and walk with Jesus, life feels good.

THINGS I WOULD TELL MY YOUNGER SELF

*"**Make Jesus your best friend.** He is the one you can count on no matter what. He always has what's best for you and He teaches you how to be a great friend to others. You will still make other wonderful friendships along the way, but make Jesus #1."*

SEE IT — STOP IT — START IT

1. What part of life are you trying to do on your own?

2. What would it feel like to have Jesus as your best friend?

3. Why does walking with Jesus make life easier and give you rest for your soul?

What do you **SEE?** _____

_____

What are you going to **STOP?** _____

_____

What are you going to **START?** _____

_____

Key Verses: Psalm 23:1-3, Matthew 16:24

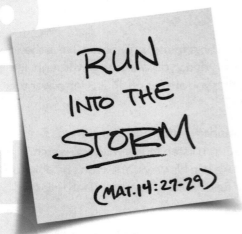

RUN
INTO THE
STORM
(MAT.14:27-29)

Jesus immediately said to them: 'Take courage! It is I. Don't be afraid.' 'Lord, if it's you,' Peter replied, 'tell me to come to you on the water.' 'Come,' He said. Then Peter got down out of the boat, walked on the water and came toward Jesus.

– Matthew 14:27-29

GRACE'S STORY

"I've loved thunderstorms ever since I can remember. My Dad would take us to the front porch so we could see the lightning and feel the thunder! Many times, I would run out into the rain and splash in the puddles. I've learned that life brings a lot of storms and how you approach the storm – with faith or fear – matters a lot. Being ready for them and even enjoying them is a lot better than being afraid."

GET STRONG

Most people are afraid of thunderstorms. Sometimes you can even feel those loud rumbles of thunder and cracks of lightening. Sometimes you see storms coming and other times you get surprised by them. But one thing is certain, storms will come.

In Colorado, cows and bison roam freely in close proximity to one another. Cows and bison are similar, but how they react to storms is very different.

The cows see the storm coming and scatter. They run away in fear, hoping they can avoid the storm, but in the end, it always catches them. Their fearful running keeps them in the storm longer, extending their pain and discomfort.

The bison see the storm and run into it. They come together as a herd and run straight into the storm. They shorten the time spent in the storm and reduce the negative impact. By staying together, they defeat the fear and overcome it.

Peter, one of Jesus' closest friends, was famous for getting out of the safety of the boat and walking on water straight into the storm. As long as he kept his eyes on Jesus, he walked with confidence and faith. When he worried about the storm, he sank.

The storms in your life might be a failure, an illness, a disappointment, or a big life change. They might bring doubts, anxiety, or worry. Whether you see it coming or it comes as a surprise, face it with faith. Don't run from it in fear.

Confidently face the storm with faith in the God of the winds and waves. Come together with other believers and weather storms together. Run into the storm.

THINGS I WOULD TELL MY YOUNGER SELF

"Face the storms of life, don't run from them. Trying to avoid pain, difficulties, conflict, or consequences for your actions just makes it worse. Take ownership and responsibility and do what you can to learn, grow, or resolve the situation. Ignoring it won't make it go away."

SEE IT — STOP IT — START IT

1. What storms are you facing?

2. What are ways you might face the storm head on and trust God to help?

3. How can you rely on others and God to help you weather the storm?

What do you **SEE?** _____

_____

What are you going to **STOP?** _____

_____

What are you going to **START?** _____

_____

Key Verses: Isaiah 43:2, Psalm 107:28-30, Matthew 7:24-27

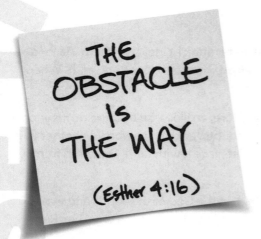

THE OBSTACLE IS THE WAY

(Esther 4:16)

I will go to the king, even though it is against the law. And if I perish, I perish.

– Esther 4:16

GRACE'S STORY

"I've always been pretty fearless when it comes to tackling challenges or overcoming obstacles. But I never thought the obstacle might be exactly what God was allowing or even putting in my path to refine my character and make me better. If you see obstacles as a sign to give up, you may face more until you learn what God wants to teach you. If you look for ways to avoid them, you'll miss out on the blessings of character, confidence, and courage."

GET STRONG

Obstacle course racing (OCR) has become one of the fastest growing sports in the world. Athletes compete in distances as short as a 5k all the way to 13.1 miles or more. But what makes this sport unique is that you must clear between 20 – 32 obstacles along the way. It's a sport most of our family has grown to love.

You will encounter obstacles in every aspect of life. There will be things in the way of having healthy relationships, good health, success in school or work, and even sharing your faith. Most people see obstacles as something to be avoided. But, if you can see obstacles as opportunities for growth, they will be exactly what you need to be your best and live your faith courageously.

The story of Esther is one of overcoming obstacles to protect the Jewish people. Esther, queen of Persia, faced two huge obstacles – the risk of revealing her Jewish identity to King Xerxes and the fear of losing her life for approaching the King without permission. She faced and overcame these obstacles through prayer and fasting; it gave her the courage she needed. She stood strong for God. There was no other way to save her people. The obstacle was the way.

Jesus modeled this principle for us. His biggest obstacle was the cross, and He faced that, even enduring ridicule, shame, and physical trauma before ultimately giving up his life for all of us. He chose to go to the cross to pay the price for all our sins so that we could be reconciled to God and receive the free gift of eternal life. Before that trial, Jesus asked His Father if there was any other way, if He could remove the obstacle. But ultimately, the obstacle is the way.

THINGS I WOULD TELL MY YOUNGER SELF

"The obstacle is the way to your best life. You can't grow and get better without something to stretch you or overcome. Develop a 'bring it on!' mindset and expect God to do great things in you and through you because of the challenge."

SEE IT — STOP IT — START IT

1. What obstacles are you facing today?

2. Do you see them as something to fear, avoid, or confront head on?

3. What are some things you can do to summon the courage to overcome the obstacle?

What do you **SEE?** _____

_____

What are you going to **STOP?** _____

_____

What are you going to **START?** _____

_____

Key Verses: Romans 5:3-5, Genesis 37-50, James 1:2-4

*Be still, and know
that I am God.*

– Psalm 46:10

GRACE'S STORY

*"When I was competing on the athletic field, I had no problem staying
focused and ignoring the noise from the crowd or even my opponents.
Trash talk never bothered me. But the noise from me 'getting in my own
head' and ruminating on things I was fearful or anxious about – that was
a different story altogether. My Dad's voice was the only voice I could hear
that would break through."*

GET STRONG

We live in a world that is really noisy. Most of the noise consists of
criticism, negativity, and comparison that can make you feel anxious,
overwhelmed, and discouraged. God has the antidote for the noise –
Be still.

During the Olympic games in Tokyo, Simone Biles – the world's best
gymnast – felt overwhelming pressure to lead Team USA to the gold
medal. So much so that she experienced "the twisties" where she
couldn't tell up from down during her routine. This can be dangerous, as it
presents a real risk of serious injury, given that so much of gymnastics is
spent "in the air."

When she decided to withdraw from the Olympics, the negative noise
got very loud. The greatest gymnast in the world was called a quitter.
With the help of her teammates, she ignored the noise and focused on
the truth. In the end, she overcame the noise, competed in one last event
and earned the bronze medal.

Everyone faces noise. And with social media, it can be overwhelmingly loud. But God gives you a simple way to ignore it, quiet your mind and spirit, and experience peace. He tells you to simply 'be still' and remember that God is good and He's in control. When you pause and focus on God, you can hear His still, small voice whispering the truth over the noise. That brings peace.

Jesus endured a lot of noise. The Pharisees constantly challenged Him and tried to trap Him. The devil tried to tempt Him when He was weak, tired, and hungry. People mocked Him and even insulted Him. But He could ignore the noise. How? By going to a quiet place, getting still, and focusing on His Father's Voice. Turn off the noise and tune in to God. Be still.

THINGS I WOULD TELL MY YOUNGER SELF

*"**Be still and turn off the noise.** Focus on hearing God's Voice above all the others and trust it. Focus on your breathing and silently saying God's word as you breathe in and out. Breath in – 'The Lord is my shepherd.' Breathe out – 'I have everything I need.' This works to help quiet your mind and spirit."*

SEE IT — STOP IT — START IT

1. What is causing all the noise in your life?

2. How does the noise make you feel?

3. What can you do right now to be still, turn off the noise, and tune in to God?

What do you **SEE?** _____

_____

What are you going to **STOP?** _____

_____

What are you going to **START?** _____

_____

Key Verses: Proverbs 4:25-27, Hebrews 12:1-2, Matthew 5:11-12

DON'T WORRY BE HAPPY! :)

(Phil. 4:6-7)

Do not be anxious about anything, but in every situation, by prayer and petition, with thanksgiving, present your requests to God. And the peace of God, which transcends all understanding, will guard your hearts and your minds in Christ Jesus.

– Philippians 4:6-7

GRACE'S STORY

"I truly want to be happy. I don't know anyone who'd rather be sad or miserable. Life is a gift, and it's meant to be enjoyed. Even though it can be hard and bad things happen, God truly wants you to have peace and joy, no matter the circumstances. I worried a lot about friendships and being liked and it robbed me of being happy until I finally decided to look for the bright side, pray, ask, and trust God. My attitude and even my moods improved!"

GET STRONG

American musician Bobby McFerrin wrote the #1 hit song "Don't Worry, Be Happy" way back in 1988! It's one of those songs that just makes you smile. He conveys the truth that worry brings you down and makes things worse. It never makes things better.

Lots of things cause anxiety, worry and fear today. Most of what we're worried about never happens. We think things are going to be worse than they end up being. It takes effort to see the bright-side. That's why God spends so much time encouraging us to give all our cares to Him, because He takes care of us.

Worrying doesn't help us, ever; not even a little bit. All it does is rob us of enjoying life right now. It can't make your life better; it won't solve your problems; it won't improve your energy or your attitude. And worry is even bad for your emotional and physical health.

The verse above is the official "don't worry, be happy" verse in the Bible. It's not just a cute thing to say; the verse tells you exactly what to do to stop worrying, trust God, and enjoy peace. Instead of worrying about how things will work out, be thankful for every situation, pray, and ask God for what you want.

When you release it to God, He takes the burden and gives you peace. Now that's a pretty good deal. But the secret of this process is to trust that God will work it out for your good and His glory, even if it's not quite like you wanted.

So, give it a try. Don't worry, be happy.

THINGS I WOULD TELL MY YOUNGER SELF

*"**Don't Worry, be Happy!** This one is so good, just do what the post-it says! When you pray, and give everything to God, He guards your heart and mind and gives you peace. Peace brings happiness!"*

SEE IT — STOP IT — START IT

1. What are some things you are worried or anxious about right now?

2. Take a minute to pray and ask God to help you and resolve it.

3. Then, say "Don't worry, be happy!" out loud and enjoy the peace from trusting God.

What do you **SEE?** _____

_____

What are you going to **STOP?** _____

_____

What are you going to **START?** _____

_____

Key Verses: Matthew 6:25-34, 1 Peter 5:7, Psalm 55:22

STAY
PURE
(Prov. 4:23)

Above all else, guard your heart, for everything you do flows from it.

– Proverbs 4:23

GRACE'S STORY

"I faced so much pressure against purity. I got sucked into social media and played the comparison game. It created a lot of insecurity. The pressure to do things to fit in or be liked was intense, so I did things I normally wouldn't. While that brought me temporary happiness, it ultimately led me into anxiety and depression. I finally realized I was more valuable than I was being treated and the choices I was making. I just got tired of not holding to my standard and began honoring God with my words and actions."

GET STRONG

Purity is a virtue. It means you are free from contamination because you hold to a righteous standard of behavior. Purity always leads to a lightness of heart, healthy relationships, inner peace, and personal wellbeing. It genuinely feels so good when you never have to worry that you'll be embarrassed by something you're doing or saying if others ever found out about it.

Purity originates from goodness, including good intentions, motives, thoughts, words, and actions. There's no doubt that staying pure is a tough challenge with all the negative and impure influences and temptations all around you. It's hard to go against the flow.

There are many ways to stay pure, but it's only possible if you live according to God's Word. Knowing God's intention for you and learning in the bible about the things that lead to a pure life helps you do those things.

Staying pure starts with guarding your heart because everything you do or say reflects the condition of your heart. You do that by protecting your eyes from seeing inappropriate things and staying focused on what is good, honorable, and uplifting. Your phone may be your biggest problem to solve. You also do that by being careful what you say. God encourages you to not use foul language because it damages your heart. And last, be careful where you go because it could put you in a compromising situation.

Remember, there's no such thing as a perfect person. No one will be perfectly pure, so don't put that pressure on yourself. But the pursuit of purity is worth it. If you fall short, it's important to admit it and resolve to do better next time; learn what you can and take steps to prevent that mistake in the future. Purity leads to freedom and life. Stay pure.

THINGS I WOULD TELL MY YOUNGER SELF

"Fitting in or being liked isn't worth the cost of compromise. *It never lasts. Realize how valuable you are in God's eyes and expect others to treat you accordingly. Never compromise just to be liked. You will never regret staying pure."*

SEE IT — STOP IT — START IT

1. What are practical ways you can protect your purity?

2. Where are you most vulnerable? What can you do to avoid compromising situations?

3. How can you recover when you fail?

What do you **SEE?** _____

_____

What are you going to **STOP?** _____

_____

What are you going to **START?** _____

_____

Key Verses: Psalm 119:9, Matthew 26:41, 1 John 1:9, 1 Corinthians 9:27

LITTLE THINGS
LEAD TO
BIG THINGS
(Mat 25:21)

'Well done, good and faithful servant! You have been faithful with a few things; I will put you in charge of many things. Come and share your master's happiness!'

– Matthew 25:21

GRACE'S STORY

*"When I was little, me and my brothers used to watch a VeggieTales©
cartoon episode called 'Larry-Boy! & the Fib from Outer Space!'. Every
time Junior Asparagus tells a little lie; Fib grows bigger and bigger until he
takes over the entire town. Even though it was just a cartoon, I learned
the lesson that little things lead to big things. Whether it's eating right,
studying, and serving or lies, excuses, and compromises, both grow, for
better or worse."*

GET STRONG

It's fun to set up dominoes and then watch as they all fall one by one after
you push the first one over. Each domino can knock over the next domino
1.5 times its size. If you start with a tiny domino just 5mm tall and line up 28
more dominoes, each one 1.5 times bigger and heavier, the last domino it
knocks over would be the height of the Empire State Building in New York.

The little things that we do (or don't do) every day add up. Every decision,
action, thought, and word counts. Life is all about small decisions.

One little excuse or compromise never seems like a big deal and most
of the time doesn't seem to matter. But one excuse usually leads to
the next, bigger excuse. One compromise makes it easier to make a
bigger compromise. These little things add up over time and produce
disappointing results.

On the positive side, one good decision, one promise kept, one act of
kindness leads to the next and produces positive results. These things
shape your character.

In the parable of the talents in Mathew 25, three people were given responsibility to take care of some money. Two of them completed the necessary tasks to multiply the money they were given, while one did nothing. In the end, the two who were faithful with the little things were trusted with big things. The one who acted out of fear ended up with nothing.

It's the little things done behind the scenes – reading your bible, exercising, eating the right foods, studying, serving – that result in really big things like strong faith, good health, success, and a satisfying life. Little things always lead to big things.

THINGS I WOULD TELL MY YOUNGER SELF

"The little things add up. Small choices and decisions seem so insignificant at the time so you may not care. But if you could see how those choices stack up and eventually may cause a big problem, it would most likely change your choice now."

SEE IT — STOP IT — START IT

1. What little things are you doing that might add up to a big, negative thing?

2. What little things are you doing that might add up to a big, positive thing?

3. What's one thing you would stop (and start) that could change your direction?

What do you **SEE?** _____

_____

What are you going to **STOP?** _____

_____

What are you going to **START?** _____

_____

Key Verses: Matthew 13:31-32, Proverbs 13:11, James 3:5

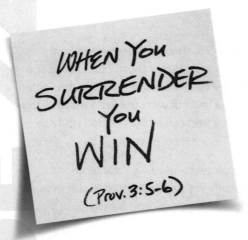

WHEN YOU SURRENDER You WIN

(Prov. 3:5-6)

Trust in the Lord with all your heart and lean not on your own understanding; in all your ways submit to him, and He will make your paths straight.

– Proverbs 3:5-6

GRACE'S STORY

"I tend to want to control things. As a competitive person, the idea of 'surrendering to win' was a hard concept to grasp. So much of life is out of our control; we just think we're in control. When I realized that God is in charge, and that He always wants what's best for me, it made it easier to let go and trust Him with the results. I'm way more joyful and way less stressful when I release the outcome to God."

GET STRONG

A parable tells the story of two teams engaged in a battle of tug-o-war. Each team gripped the rope and pulled with all their might. As the competition wore on, one team realized they were destined to lose, so they agreed to release the rope and surrender the match. On the count of three, they let go, sending the other team tumbling to victory. The 'losing' team jumped up and down, celebrating as they no longer had the struggle of hanging on.

This parable illustrates the power of surrender. The team that let go of the rope was hanging on to control, resentment, and unforgiveness. By releasing the rope, it appeared they lost, but they won a great victory of freedom and healing.

You may want to control as much of your life as possible. But that's like hanging on tightly to the rope. You think it gives you the best chance to win, but all it does is exhaust you.

The secret to life is surrender. Before He was crucified, Jesus perfectly modeled this by praying, "Father, if you are willing, take this cup from me; yet not my will, but yours be done." Through surrender, He won the victory over sin and death, offering eternal life to all who believe.

Surrendering your plans, hopes, and dreams to your Heavenly Father requires that you trust Him. It brings freedom and joy and peace.

God has grand plans for you. It won't be all sunshine and rainbows. But when you surrender control and trust in the Lord with all your heart, He will make your path straight. When you ask God for wisdom and direction, it gives you indescribable confidence. No matter what life brings, God will give you everything you need to thrive. When you surrender, you win.

THINGS I WOULD TELL MY YOUNGER SELF

"Control is an illusion. The more you try to control everything, the less you enjoy your life. Peace and joy come when you surrender everyone and everything to God."

SEE IT — STOP IT — START IT

1. What aspects of your life are you trying to control by "hanging onto the rope"?

2. How do you feel when things don't go your way or you can't control them?

3. What do you need to surrender to God and trust Him with?

What do you **SEE?** _____

_____

What are you going to **STOP?** _____

_____

What are you going to **START?** _____

_____

Key Verses: Luke 22:42, Galatians 2:20, James 4:7, Matthew 16:24

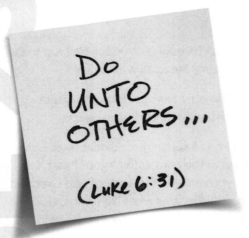

Do unto others as you would have them do unto you.

– Luke 6:31

GRACE'S STORY

"It's so easy to treat others well when they are treating you well. But it's super challenging when you're being left out, gossiped about, or mistreated. My natural response in those moments is to get defensive; that never seems to make things better. You can only experience true freedom when your response is not influenced by how you are being treated. Extending grace and kindness diffuses anger and conflict."

GET STRONG

The "Golden Rule" – Do unto others as you would have them do unto you – is one of the most well-known sayings in the world. Almost everyone has heard of it across countries and cultures. It is a guiding light for many families and cultures.

Here's what it means – In any given situation, ask yourself what you would want people to do for you, then take the initiative and do that for them.

It is truly the simplest principle to know and understand, but it can be one of the most difficult to do. Unfortunately, things get in the way and stop you from doing this. Pressure from friends to exclude someone, gossiping about a classmate, or just not taking the time to help someone who obviously needs help are a few examples.

The parable of the Good Samaritan in Luke 10 is a great illustration. In this story, robbers attacked a man and badly hurt him. First, religious people passed by without offering help. Finally, another man came to his aid and rescued him. He must have had the "Golden Rule" in his heart and asked what he would want someone to do for him if the roles were reversed.

How would he want to be treated in a similar situation?

Once you realize you will someday need help, you will become much more excited about helping others in need. It helps you understand everyone goes through similar challenges and probably feels the same way.

Can you imagine if everyone all at once just followed this rule? It might just be the best day ever! You have the power within you to take responsibility for how you treat others and to model this for your friends.

When you treat others this way, it always comes back to you. Do unto others.

THINGS I WOULD TELL MY YOUNGER SELF

"Treat others well, regardless of how you feel. By modeling how Jesus would respond and what He would do, you may point people to His grace, goodness, and kindness. Conflict is unlikely to do that."

SEE IT — STOP IT — START IT

1. Why can it be so hard to do unto others? To treat them as you want to be treated?

2. What gets in the way?

3. What will you do to make this part of who you are?

What do you **SEE?** _____

_____

What are you going to **STOP?** _____

_____

What are you going to **START?** _____

_____

Key Verses: Colossians 3:12, 1 Peter 3:8, Ephesians 4:32

FORGIVEN MEANS FORGOTTEN

(Psalm 103:12)

As far as the east is from the west, so far has He removed our transgressions from us.

– Psalm 103:12

GRACE'S STORY

"When my parents disciplined me when I was little, they would say 'you're forgiven; it's all over...forgotten.' As I got older, my Dad would say 'and I will never bring it up again.' While I knew this was true, it was still hard to believe. God (and my parents) would literally forget my past sins and never use them against me or remind me of them again. That was not only a picture of grace, but it set me free from carrying around guilt and shame."

GET STRONG

Forgiveness is a decision. Jesus willingly purchased our freedom from sin and death when He took our punishment on the cross. He was sinless, yet shed His blood and sacrificed His life for our freedom.

Since you have received forgiveness, you must extend forgiveness to others. God also expects you to humbly ask for forgiveness when you've wronged someone else. Sometimes it's easy, and other times it's hard, depending upon how serious the issue was.

Some have a hard time forgiving God for things that have happened to them. Sometimes, you may feel tempted to hold on to unforgiveness to punish the other person or assert control. But when we withhold forgiveness, everybody loses. The destructive emotions of bitterness, anger, and resentment burden us, and the relationship stays damaged. If this condition lasts for too long, it could destroy the relationship.

The passage in Psalms 103 shows us how God forgives – completely. He removes your sin and remembers it no more. He loves you that much. Love and forgiveness have no limits. Now the enemy will try to bring up past mistakes and get you to feel guilt and shame all over again. He tries to make you bring your past into the present to steal your joy today.

If you let the devil remind you of the sins that God has already forgiven you for, you are disrespecting His sacrifice. God chooses to forget your sins; you should too. Thank Jesus for the sin debt that was canceled at the cross of Calvary, and move on!

That gift must motivate you to pass on the same measure of forgiveness to others. Don't hold past sins over anyone's head. God doesn't and you shouldn't either. Set them free.

What God forgives, He forgets.

THINGS I WOULD TELL MY YOUNGER SELF

*"**Forget the past**. Leave it far behind you and don't let the enemy bring it into your present. If he tries, just say 'Satan, God has forgiven and forgotten and I do too.' And make sure you offer that same forgiveness to others."*

SEE IT — STOP IT — START IT

1. What are you hanging onto that Jesus has already forgiven you for?

2. Who do you need to ask for forgiveness from or extend forgiveness to?

3. How is holding on to the past hurting you now?

What do you **SEE?** _____

_____

What are you going to **STOP?** _____

_____

What are you going to **START?** _____

_____

Key Verses: Micah 7:18-19, 1 John 1:9, Hebrews 8:12, Psalm 32:1-2, Colossians 3:13

No
PRESSURE
NO
DIAMONDS

(1 Pet. 4:12-13)

Dear friends, do not be surprised at the fiery ordeal that has come on you to test you, as though something strange were happening to you. But rejoice inasmuch as you participate in the sufferings of Christ, so that you may be overjoyed when his glory is revealed.

– 1 Peter 4:12-13

GRACE'S STORY

"I used to feel pressure before tests in school, a big game in lacrosse, or a big decision like what college to attend. I didn't want to fail. Pressure can cause anxiety and can be overwhelming. It wasn't until I saw pressure as something that could help me grow or make me perform at my best that it changed. I said 'I'm better under pressure' whenever I felt the anxiety."

GET STRONG

You will face pressure in life. You may face it in the classroom for a big test, on the playing field, or with something that is tempting you to compromise your standard. Some of you avoid stress at all costs because it stresses you out. Others thrive under it and even enjoy it.

Depending on how you see the stress, it can be very positive and beneficial. The best athletes talk about how they need pressure to perform at their best. It turns out that there is an optimal level of stress that gets you to be your best. Too much pressure and you get overwhelmed. Too little and you get lazy. How you see pressure will determine how it affects you.

It's impossible to develop character and peak performance, or even maturity, without adversity and pressure. People that have the most wisdom and make the best decisions have almost always experienced great pressure and adversity and weathered those storms.

Pressure reveals and refines character. When we get squeezed, what comes out shows us what's inside. It exposes things you need to change and gives you a chance to let God refine you.

God forges our character, confidence, and courage the same way He forms diamonds. A single element, Carbon, forms diamonds. Carbon is soft, but after going through the process, it becomes invincible. It takes time, extreme heat, and pressure to transform carbon into a diamond. When carbon goes deeper beneath the surface of the earth (100 miles down), it encounters extreme temperatures and pressure.

Those extreme conditions make diamonds. And when it rises again to the surface, it displays the brilliance of the light. That's the purpose of pressure – to transform you into someone who shines for Jesus. *No pressure, no diamonds.*

THINGS I WOULD TELL MY YOUNGER SELF

"See pressure as positive. Take control of your thoughts and say 'I'm better under pressure' when you feel that stress come on. It will change your perspective, your expectation, and your energy for the task."

SEE IT — STOP IT — START IT

1. Do you see pressure as something to avoid or embrace?

2. What pressures are you facing right now?

3. What mantra can you say to change your expectation and energy?

What do you **SEE?** _____

_____

What are you going to **STOP?** _____

_____

What are you going to **START?** _____

_____

Key Verses: 1 Peter 1:6-7, 2 Corinthians 4:17-18, James 1:2-4

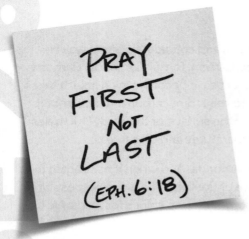

PRAY FIRST NoT LAST (EPH. 6:18)

And pray in the Spirit on all occasions with all kinds of prayers and requests. With this in mind, be alert and always keep on praying for all the Lord's people.

– Ephesians 6:18

GRACE'S STORY

"The biggest obstacle to prayer for me was that I really didn't know how to pray. I found it difficult to pray because distractions easily diverted my attention and my thoughts wandered. Or I just felt like I didn't know what to say. Praying in public was hard because I thought I had to be good at it. The only time it was easy was when I desperately needed God's help!"

GET STRONG

Jesus never meant for prayer to be something you do out of desperation alone. He doesn't want us to reach out to Him when things are going wrong. He wants to be on speed dial. He wants to be the one you text throughout the day just to check in. And He's available 24/7/365. He never takes a day off and He cares about every aspect of your life.

The Bible gives us tons of help for how, why, and when to pray. The passage above in Ephesians 6 refers to prayer as one of the spiritual weapons we have to overcome the schemes of the enemy. Here are some keys to prayer from that passage:

- Pray under the guidance of the Holy Spirit. Ask God to bring specific things and people to mind.

- Pray all the time in all circumstances, not just when you think you need God's help.

- Pray for what you need, what you're thankful for, and for others who need help.

- Pray for the wellbeing and strength of other believers.

- Pray to be ready for the attacks of the enemy.

Prayer is designed to be an ongoing, Spirit-led discipline. Jesus modeled that prayer is to be a priority for you. He specifically gave you words to pray in the Lord's Prayer. He taught you to pray daily, pray early in the morning, continually, and about everything! That's a pretty good blueprint!

Don't wait until you're in trouble to call upon God. Keep the line of communication open at all times. He's ready to listen and answer!

THINGS I WOULD TELL MY YOUNGER SELF

"Don't wait to pray. Use prayer as an offensive weapon, not defensive. Take territory for God. You have direct access to the God of all Creation and He wants you to talk to Him! Prayer is just a conversation. Don't wait to ask Him for direction or help until you are in a mess. Don't worry about having all the right words or sounding good. Pray early and often!"

SEE IT — STOP IT — START IT

1. Is your natural first step to pray or act?

2. Do you keep open lines of communication with God or just when you need Him?

3. Consider using the Lord's Prayer as a place to start.

What do you **SEE?** _____

_____

What are you going to **STOP?** _____

_____

What are you going to **START?** _____

_____

Key Verses: Matthew 6:9-13, 1 Thess. 5:16-18, Colossians 4:2,
   Mark 1:35, James 5:13, Phil. 4:6

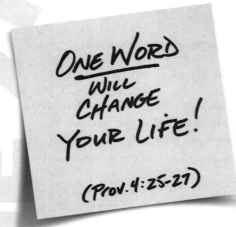

One Word
WILL
CHANGE
YouR LiFE!

(Prov. 4:25-27)

Let your eyes look straight ahead... Do not turn to the right or the left.

– Proverbs 4:25-27

GRACE'S STORY

"Since before I was born, my family has been picking One Word to focus on for the year, and my Dad's involvement as one of the authors of the One Word book has made us totally committed. In high school I got more serious about it, expecting God to bring positive change into my life. The most transformative word I chose was 'Surrender'. I had to 'let go' of control and trust God. 'Surrender' changed my mind, my heart, my emotions, my spirit, and my actions."

GET STRONG

Since 1999, we've been discovering our *One Word* themes for the year. We used to make New Year's resolutions, but that never worked! We started with good intentions, but finished the year where we started. Resolutions are about what you hope to get done; *One Word* is about who you want to become.

By narrowing the focus to just *One Word*, we've discovered the secret to life-change. The simplicity of focusing on *One Word* for the year brings clarity and intentionality and keeps you focused on what matters most.

You can discover your one word in three simple steps:

1. **Look In:** Prepare your heart. Eliminating noise and distractions properly prepares the heart to hear from God about what you need most.

2. **Look Up:** Discover your word. When you ask God to reveal your *One Word* and listen, He gives you the word meant for you.

3. **Look Out:** Live your word. Keep your one word front and center throughout the year. Share it with your inner circle of friends and family. Live your word to its fullest.

Jesus modeled the power of focus. He was never in a hurry or controlled by others. He had a mission and refused to be distracted along the way.

One Word has changed our entire family. *One Word* will change the way you think, the words you speak, the attitudes of your heart, your relationships, and even your actions. We've had words like Do, Sunrises, Brave, Strong, Unstoppable, Kind, Miracles, Discipline, Thankful, Peace, Trust, Listen, Pray, Positive, Shine, and many more.

If you were to focus on *One Word* that could have the greatest positive impact on you, what would it be? What's your *One Word?*

THINGS I WOULD TELL MY YOUNGER SELF

"Don't just pick a word, ask God to give you a word. Get the One Word book and go through the process. Then take it seriously and expect God to transform you from the inside out."

SEE IT — STOP IT — START IT

1. Go through the *One Word* process to discover your *One Word* for the year.

2. Share your *One Word* and discuss the reasons why you chose it.

3. Put your *One Word* front and center; stay focused on life-change.

What do you **SEE?** _____

_____

What are you going to **STOP?** _____

_____

What are you going to **START?** _____

_____

Key Verses: Philippians 3:13-14, Mark 10:21, John 9:25

> "Am I now trying to win the approval of human beings, or of God? Or am I trying to please people? If I were still trying to please people, I would not be a servant of Christ."
>
> – Galatians 1:10

GRACE'S STORY

"I have always felt pressure to make other people happy. The pressure to fit in or the desire to be liked is real. It's uncomfortable sometimes to go against the flow or do things differently. And sometimes you just don't want to stand out because you know how people are going to react. But standing up for God and living up to your standard is worth it."

GET STRONG

There's a saying, 'If you chase two rabbits, both will escape.' Our dogs try this and whenever two rabbits are on the scene, their pursuit is hopeless. They simply cannot have success with divided attention.

You are probably familiar with the term 'people-pleasers.' The desire to want to make other people happy is normal. You probably want to be liked, so it can be easier to just go along with the crowd than take a different path.

But if trying to please others causes you to not please God, or to disobey what He is asking you to do, that becomes a problem. At that point, you have a choice to make. Will you obey God or make others happy? We all face this situation at one time or another.

In the verse above, the apostle Paul knew this principle well. He knew there would be times when he would have to choose between pleasing God and pleasing people. He couldn't chase both rabbits. He knew that if he tried to please people, he could not be a servant of Christ. At some point, he would have to tell people truth they would not like or might have to challenge them.

Pleasing people instead of God will never give you a sense of peace and joy. When your intention is to please God and follow His purpose for your life, your priorities become clear and your heart becomes undivided. Single-minded focus on Jesus gives you the power to stay on track and keep your mind and heart set on things above.

When you face a choice between pleasing God or pleasing people, please God. You can never go wrong.

THINGS I WOULD TELL MY YOUNGER SELF

"It's impossible to make everybody happy all the time. But when you choose to obey God and do things His way, it's always best for you. It's good for your mind and heart. You may not please everybody, but they will probably respect your decisions."

SEE IT — STOP IT — START IT

1   Are you afraid to let other people down?

2.   Give an example when you've had to choose who to please, God or people.

3.   How does it feel when you choose to do it God's way?

What do you **SEE?** _____

_____

What are you going to **STOP?** _____

_____

What are you going to **START?** _____

_____

Key Verses: Ephesians 6:6-7, Acts 5:29, Colossians 3:23-24, 1 Thess. 2:4, Romans 12:1

SMILE

(Prov. 15:13)

*A happy heart makes
the face cheerful.*

– Proverbs 15:13

GRACE'S STORY

*"I like people who smile a lot. I guess they're just more fun to be around.
It doesn't mean they're always happy, because no one is. But I've found
they are more positive, optimistic, and joyful most of the time. Plus, when
someone smiles at me, it's contagious. It makes me want to smile, and it
lifts my mood. We are all contagious, so let's be positively contagious."*

GET STRONG

A warm and genuine smile can light up a room. Genuinely happy people
can transform the energy around them with their presence. Happy people
are magnetic; they draw others to them. You want to be around them. It's
not by chance; your countenance affects how others experience you.

It's hard not to wear your emotion on your face. In fact, your facial
expressions are often a reflection of your heart. If you are sad or mad,
your face will let others know.

When your heart is happy, it shines through your expressions and
energy, making your face cheerful. This joy is genuine; it's rooted in your
relationship with God, not in your circumstances. A happy heart inside
shows up on the outside.

If you don't feel so happy and want a happy heart, start by counting your
blessings. A thankful heart makes you focus on what's going right and
what matters most. Whenever you feel a bit off, take a moment to think
of what you're thankful for.

It also helps to listen to worship music. Hearing spirit-filled words in song

EXERCISE 29

can lift your spirits. Adding brief prayers as you listen, or singing along helps you experience His presence, which is fullness of joy (Psalm 16:11).

Amazingly, just as a cheerful heart can put a smile on your face, the opposite is also true. Smiling can help give you a cheerful heart! Smiling actually changes your physiology by releasing hormones that make you happy. God's design is miraculous. So, when your heart is feeling heavy, smile. Imagine the joy you can spread just by wearing a smile on your face!

Happiness is not only an internal state. It's also a result of what you do. Intentionally serving others and being kind spreads happiness. Whether it's helping a neighbor, volunteering, or simply being a good friend, these actions not only bring happiness to others, but also fill your heart with joy. And that joy always shows up on your face. Smile!

THINGS I WOULD TELL MY YOUNGER SELF

"Smile, even when you don't feel like it. It's easy to become so serious and forget that life is meant to be enjoyed. Pick your head up and smile a big smile. Your smiling face might be exactly what someone needs to see!"

SEE IT — STOP IT — START IT

1 Does smiling come naturally to you?

2. How can a smile from someone else brighten your day?

3. Is your facial expression a reflection of your heart?

What do you **SEE?** _____

_____

What are you going to **STOP?** _____

_____

What are you going to **START?** _____

_____

Key Verses: Proverbs 15:30, Proverbs 17:22, Ecclesiastes 8:1, Psalm 19:8, Proverbs 16:15

SHOW ME YOUR
FRIENDS
I'LL SHOW YOU
YOUR
FUTURE
(Prov. 13:20)

Walk with the wise and become wise, for a companion of fools suffers harm.

– Proverbs 13:20

GRACE'S STORY

"The most powerful 'outside' influences are friends. At some point, I cared more about what my friends thought than almost anybody else. This became a big problem when my friends were pitting me against my parents and encouraging me to say and do things I would not normally say or do. I went along and it didn't go very well for me. There is no more important decision than who your friends are. It will direct the future you."

GET STRONG

Friends will make or break you. They will make you a better person or break you down into someone who's less than you should be. Friends are a powerful force in your life, so it's incredibly important how you choose your friends. Show me your friends and I will show you your future. That's the level of influence they can have in your life.

The verse above says it best, "He who walks with the wise grows wise, but a companion of fools suffers harm." Friends are not neutral in your life; they will either help you or hurt you. There is no middle ground. You want friends in your life who make you better.

They won't be perfect, of course, because nobody's perfect. But they should be moving in the same direction you are. If there's a lot of drama surrounding friends – like conflict or gossip – you probably want to rethink your friend group.

Here are three questions you can ask to figure out if your friends should be your friends – Do they follow Jesus? Do they do the right thing? Are they trustworthy and kind? In addition, are they encouraging you to:

1. Grow in your relationship with Jesus?

2. Hold to a high personal standard of behavior?

3. Develop habits that lead to optimal health and wellbeing?

4. Love and respect your parents and family?

These are some basic qualities you should look for in friends. And, this is an excellent guide for the type of friend you should be for others. You will have friends – like classmates, teammates, roommates – who don't meet these basic criteria, but you may not want them as your closest friends.

When you're moving in the right direction, you attract other friends who are moving in the same direction. You can help your friends fulfill their potential; they can do the same for you. Your friends will shape your future, so choose wisely.

THINGS I WOULD TELL MY YOUNGER SELF

"Choose your friends for their character, not popularity. One genuine, trustworthy, loyal friend is more valuable than 100 fake friends. Be a real friend and find real friends."

SEE IT – STOP IT – START IT

1 Who are your real friends?

2. What are the most important qualities of great friends?

3. In what ways do friends affect your future?

What do you **SEE?** _____

_____

What are you going to **STOP?** _____

_____

What are you going to **START?** _____

_____

Key Verses: 1 Corinthians 15:33, Proverbs 12:26, Proverbs 27:17

For though we live in the world, we do not wage war as the world does. The weapons we fight with are not the weapons of the world. On the contrary, they have divine power to demolish strongholds.

– 2 Corinthians 10:3-4

GRACE'S STORY

"When my parents sensed a spirit of fear or discouragement in the house, or we were fighting a lot, they would grab the Bible, walk through the house, and speak God's Word. I saw what it looked like to go on the offense against the schemes of the devil! Now, when the enemy attacks me with lies and fear, I do what Jesus did and talk back to the Devil."

GET STRONG

The book of Daniel introduces us to a spiritual battle between angels and demons that influences things in the physical world. When Daniel prayed, God sent angels, but they were delayed because of a spiritual fight in the unseen world. God then sent the archangel Michael to win that battle and the angels got through to help Daniel.

During Jesus' 40 days of fasting in the wilderness, the enemy confronted Jesus three times and tempted Him. Jesus responded by speaking the Word of God. He also directly confronted demons, casting them out and setting people free.

God has given you spiritual armor for your protection, plus the power to demolish strongholds. The one offensive weapon is the sword of the Spirit, which is the word of God. Here are three ways to talk back to the devil out loud and win the spiritual battle:

1. **Speak truth to the lies.** The enemy is great at making you feel bad, small, and weak. Using God's truth brings strength – 'I am more than a conqueror in Christ' or 'God didn't give me a spirit of fear, but of power, love and a sound mind'.

2. **Speak your testimony to your trials.** Retelling the story of how Jesus saved you crushes the spirit of the enemy. Speaking of God's victory on the cross and how you have been set free, reminds you of your freedom and God's faithfulness.

3. **Speak promises to your problems.** Using God's truth gives you the victory – 'Greater is He who is in me than he who is in the world', 'No weapon formed against me shall prosper', or 'When I am weak, God is strong'.

There is power in the spoken word. Talking back to the Devil out loud brings victory.

THINGS I WOULD TELL MY YOUNGER SELF

"Speak the Word of God out loud. Use weapons in the spiritual realm where the battle is won or lost. Talking back to the devil gives you control of the conversation. Surrender to God, resist the enemy, and talk back to the devil."

SEE IT – STOP IT – START IT

1   Go back and review the enemy's strategies in chapter 5.

2.   Do you feel comfortable speaking God's truth out loud to defeat the enemy?

3.   List a few verses you can use to talk back to the enemy.

What do you **SEE?** _____

_____

What are you going to **STOP?** _____

_____

What are you going to **START?** _____

_____

Key Verses: Matthew 4:1-11, Acts 16:16-18, Ephesians 6:17, 1 Peter 5:8-9, Revelation 12:11

BE A WARRIOR NOT A WHINER (Rom. 8:37)

No, in all these things we are more than conquerors through Him who loved us.

– Romans 8:37

GRACE'S STORY

"I've always been super competitive. But I discovered when things weren't going my way, I often resorted to complaining and negativity. And that led to excuses. As an athlete, I knew my mindset and attitude would show up on the field. It also shows up in life. Whiners never win. I didn't like it when I sounded like a victim, so I knew I had to consistently choose a warrior mindset."

GET STRONG

The Bible talks a lot about conforming and transforming. Conforming means you follow along and do what everybody else is doing. Transforming means you follow God and become more and more like Jesus. All that transformation starts in your mind.

It's the think – feel – do – become loop. What you think affects how you feel. How you feel affects what you do. What you do affects who you become. So, in a very real sense, your thoughts determine your direction and destiny. Your mindset directly and indirectly determines the results you get.

Two voices compete for your attention – the Warrior and the Whiner – and both are fighting for control. As a believer, you must feed the warrior and starve the whiner. Whining never makes it better.

The whiner is consistently negative. It's full of complaints, pessimism, and problems. It plays the victim. The whiner voice wants you to lose. When the going gets tough, the whiner gets loud. This voice reminds you of all the reasons you can't and you won't. The whiner whispers in your ear, 'you're going to fail, you're not good enough, and you can't do it'. It complains about everything, makes excuses, and never takes responsibility. The whiner is resentful. It plants seeds of fear and doubt and reminds you of your failures. The whiner says can't, won't, and not now.

The warrior is consistently positive. It's full of compliments, optimism, and possibilities. It plays the victor. The warrior voice wants you to win. When the heat is on, the warrior says, 'bring it on'. This voice flips the negative into positive. It turns can't into can, won't into will, and never gives up. It encourages you to overcome obstacles and turn setbacks into comebacks. The warrior is resilient. It believes in God's power and reminds you of all the things you've overcome. The warrior says can, will, and now!

If you want to have a life of victory, silence the whiner and magnify the warrior. It takes intentionality, but this is the path to transformation.

THINGS I WOULD TELL MY YOUNGER SELF

*"**Don't be a victim.** You are a Warrior. God is for you. You are more than a conqueror in Christ Jesus. Bounce back from setbacks and say, "Bring it on!"*

SEE IT — STOP IT — START IT

1. When times are tough, what voice is louder for you?

2. How do you silence the whiner?

3. How do you feed the warrior?

What do you **SEE?** _____

_____

What are you going to **STOP?** _____

_____

What are you going to **START?** _____

_____

Key Verses: Philippians 4:8, 1 John 5:4-5, Romans 12:2, Philippians 4:13

In the same way, let your light shine before others, that they may see your good deeds and glorify your Father in heaven.

– Matthew 5:16

GRACE'S STORY

"The idea of God having specific things He wants me to do makes Him incredibly personal to me. He must know me (and you) well! It also means that He's created all of us with purpose. I found that the fastest way to feel better about myself was by doing something good for someone else. Bless and serve others. It works every time."

GET STRONG

When you keep your head down and focus on yourself, it's likely that your emotions will follow suit – going down. When all you're worried about is yourself and your life, it's easy to think that the world revolves around you.

If you spend most of your time obsessing about whether people like you or if you are wearing the right clothes or are part of the right group, it's easy to get down under the pressure. And if life isn't going your way, it's easy to get discouraged.

The fastest way to feel good is to do good. If you find yourself worried or anxious or down, it's usually because you need to take your eyes off yourself and make a positive difference for someone else. Your purpose is to do good works specifically designed for you to do along the way.

You are here to make a positive impact on others, even when you don't have it all together. Don't shrink back when you don't feel perfect. No one is perfect and you can't wait until you feel perfect to be a blessing to others.

Doing good things for others, even if they don't know you've done it, gets your eyes off your own "troubles". It lifts your mood. And, even if unnoticed or unappreciated, the satisfaction comes simply from obeying God and doing good.

The things you do every day, no matter how small they may seem, are part of a greater plan and a bigger story. Every day you have opportunities to let your light shine, be your best, and make other people's day. If you don't, who will? This makes your life invaluable. So even when your life doesn't feel like it's going your way, remember, when you do good, you feel good too.

THINGS I WOULD TELL MY YOUNGER SELF

"Get your eyes off yourself and the things you are worried about; every day ask God to show you the good things He has planned for you to do. Ask Him to give you specific names of people to bless or ways you can serve someone who needs help. If you feel down, doing good things will pick you up."

SEE IT — STOP IT — START IT

1. What are some "good things" you can do for others?

2. Why does it make you feel better when you do something good for someone else?

3. How does it make you feel knowing that God has things He's planned for you to do?

What do you **SEE?** _____

_____

What are you going to **STOP?** _____

_____

What are you going to **START?** _____

_____

Key Verses: Galatians 6:9, Titus 3:8, 1 Peter 2:12, Eph. 2:10

Go
AGAINST
THE
FLOW
(Rom 12:1)

Don't conform any longer to the pattern of this world.

– Romans 12:1

GRACE'S STORY

"I love the beach; and, I love to surf. I can't tell you how many times after an hour of surfing I've found myself way down the beach-line, far from where I started. If you've ever been playing in the water, you know how the current carries you. You must intentionally resist the pull of the current. The same is true in life. You must go against the currents of the culture to follow Jesus."

GET STRONG

Following the crowd is easy. Why? Because you experience acceptance and belonging. But if you're compromising your values to go along and belong, you'll feel an inner conflict that won't go away.

The currents of culture don't take you closer to Jesus. They pull you away from God's design and His best for your life.

Sometimes these currents are subtle; you may not even be aware you're drifting down shore or out to sea. They represent small compromises you make that the enemy says are 'no big deal'. Since they rarely result in immediate consequences, they're easy to ignore. But it doesn't take long before you realize you are way off track.

Other times, they are harsh and obvious, like a riptide. A riptide is a strong current that pulls directly away from the shore. It poses a significant threat to swimmers and surfers because of its power; it can carry you out to deep water in just moments. Swimming against a riptide is impossible. Instead, you escape by swimming parallel to the shoreline until you're out of the current, then make your way back to shore.

Peer pressure is real and can be intense. You may choose to compromise and conform under the pressure to do what everybody else is doing, wearing, or saying.

You may catch the current of a bad attitude, gossip, or poor decisions. God warns you to 'not conform' to what everyone else is doing. God's ways always lead to life. And He gives you the way to escape by renewing your mind and resisting temptation. The currents pull everyone, but you have everything you need to go against the flow and live a life of godliness.

When you identify with Jesus, your life points others to Him. And that's the purpose of godly living. Your life in Christ should be obvious to others.

Strong Girls are called to obey God and go against the flow.

THINGS I WOULD TELL MY YOUNGER SELF

"It's good to be different. *It's empowering when you choose God's way and to be uniquely you. Why do you want to be just like everybody else, anyway?"*

SEE IT — STOP IT — START IT

1   What are subtle currents at work in your life that cause drift?

2.   What are obvious currents you could get caught up in that cause destruction?

3.   How can you renew your mind and resist temptation to go against the flow?

What do you **SEE?** _____

_____

What are you going to **STOP?** _____

_____

What are you going to **START?** _____

_____

Key Verses: 2 Peter 1:3-7, 1 John 2:15-16, 1 Peter 4:4, Matthew 7:13-14

God's
GRACE
is
AMAZING
(EPH 2:8-9)

For it is by grace you have been saved, through faith—and this is not from yourselves, it is the gift of God—not by works, so that no one can boast.

– Ephesians 2:8-9

GRACE'S STORY

"Looking back on the two years where I really walked away from my faith, I see I was a lot like the 'prodigal son'. I believed the lies of the enemy that I had made too many mistakes to come back to God, but He never gave up on me and patiently waited for me to turn back to Him. When I did, He poured out His amazing grace, healing, and restoration."

GET STRONG

Amazing Grace by John Newton is one of the most famous hymns in the world. It transcends countries and cultures. You could probably sing the first verse right now – "Amazing Grace, how sweet the sound that saved a wretch like me. I once was lost, but now I'm found was blind, but now I see."

God's grace is truly amazing. God freely gives you His love, kindness, forgiveness, and mercy. You can't do anything to earn it; Jesus paid the price for your sins and reconciled you to The Father by dying on the cross and rising to new life.

You don't have to 'clean up your life' first to make yourself acceptable to God. It's not possible. That's the very reason you need grace.

The enemy wants you to believe 3 specific lies so you don't feel worthy of God's grace – you're *so bad, so lost, and so broken.* Let's tell the truth.

You're not so *bad* He can't forgive you. You may think, 'But you don't know what I've done'. There's no sin so great that God can't forgive it. Jesus wants to set you free from guilt and shame. His sacrificial love removes all sins, past, present, and future.

You're not so *lost* He can't find you. You may feel lost or confused. You may have walked away from God. But God is the Good Shepherd; He leaves the 99 to find the 1 lost sheep. He knows exactly where you are. No matter how lost you've gotten, God's love and grace will find you.

You're not so *broken* He can't fix you. You may feel like damaged goods because of mistakes you've made. You may feel hopeless. But Jesus gives hope to the hopeless. He heals the brokenhearted. There is nothing God can't fix.

He pursues you relentlessly with His amazing grace.

THINGS I WOULD TELL MY YOUNGER SELF

*"**Don't let anything keep you from coming back to Jesus.** All it takes is one decision to return and God pours out His grace upon you. He is waiting for you with open arms."*

SEE IT — STOP IT — START IT

1   Take a moment to read the parables listed below to discover the amazing grace of God.

2.   In what ways do you feel too bad, lost, or broken?

3.   In what ways have you experienced God's amazing grace?

What do you **SEE?** _____

_____

What are you going to **STOP?** _____

_____

What are you going to **START?** _____

_____

Key Verses: Luke 7:41-43, Luke 15:3-7, Luke 15:11-24, John 1:12, John 3:16, Romans 10:9

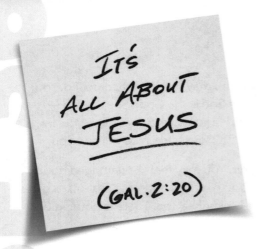

It's All About Jesus (Gal. 2:20)

I have been crucified with Christ and I no longer live, but Christ lives in me. The life I now live in the body, I live by faith in the Son of God, who loved me and gave himself for me.

– Galatians 2:20

GRACE'S STORY

"I really wanted to play lacrosse in college because it was so much of my identity and self-worth. My life revolved around being an athlete. Without that identity, I felt lost. I cared what people thought about me more than God. Once I put my identity in Christ, all the pressure to impress other people was gone. I could live to please God."

GET STRONG

One of our favorite comedians tells a joke about the "Me Monster". There's always that one person at every gathering who can't help but brag about themselves. They top everyone else's stories. They may not be aware, but selfishness, pride, and insecurity often motivate their behavior.

Many people believe this life is all about 'me'. My purpose, my truth, my way. All of that is just pride and selfishness. When you surrender your life to Jesus and receive the free gift of eternal life, you stop living for yourself and start living for Him.

You are saved by grace when you put your faith in Jesus. Nothing can separate you from the love of God. The Bible says you are now His child, part of His family, a new creation, and given a new life. You used to be under the control of the 'Me Monster', but now you are free and under the guidance of the Holy Spirit.

Your new identity is 'in Christ'. When you realize that your life is not your own, and that the Creator of the universe knows your name and has grand plans for you, it changes everything! You become unselfish, humble, and secure.

Now, you get to use all your gifts and strengths to build God's Kingdom and bring God glory. You've been called to be an ambassador for Jesus and represent Him in everything you do.

His desire is that you would be fully alive, living on purpose, doing what you're passionate about, and making a lasting difference for others. When you make it all about Jesus, your mind and heart are in sync with God.

Strong Girls flourish. A girl who is free and thriving is the epitome of beauty. It's all about Jesus.

THINGS I WOULD TELL MY YOUNGER SELF

"Don't put your identity in what you do or what you achieve. None of those things define who you are or make you important. What matters is how you're using the gifts God gave you. Are you using those things to help others and point them to Jesus or yourself?"

SEE IT — STOP IT — START IT

1   Who are you living for? Yourself or Jesus?

2. How can you use your gifts and strengths for God's glory?

3. In what ways can you make a difference for others?

What do you **SEE?** _____

_____

What are you going to **STOP?** _____

_____

What are you going to **START?** _____

_____

Key Verses: John 14:6, Colossians 1:16-17, John 15:5, Philippians 1:21, Acts 17:28, Romans 6:4

Be strong and courageous. Do not be afraid; do not be discouraged, for the Lord your God will be with you wherever you go.

– Joshua 1:9

GRACE'S STORY

"Once I got healthy and strong in my relationship with Jesus, I started living from a position of strength and victory. I don't want to be a hero, but I do want to be heroic. Who doesn't want to stand up courageously for what's right and witness God work in supernatural ways?"

GET STRONG

When asked, 'Who's the most well-known superhero?', *Superman* is the overwhelming answer. We're captivated by superheroes and every day heroes who use their physical power and moral courage to help others. In Greek mythology, a hero is known to have 'strength for two'.

No one thinks of themselves as a hero. But having a desire to be heroic is a different story. Being ready and able to act heroically and take action when the opportunity comes is part of what it means to be a *Strong Girl*.

To be heroic, you need virtuous character to put the needs of others above your own. You need confidence in yourself, and in God, that His strength will work in and through you. And you need the courage to act in the face of fear. God commands you to be strong and courageous.

Being heroic is the culmination of the *Strong Girls* journey. There are three primary opportunities you have every day to be heroic:

1. **Stand up** for what you believe, what's true, and what's right.

2. **Stand against** what's evil, wrong, and unfair.

3. **Stand with** those who are the least, last, and left out.

EXERCISE 37

You know God's Word is true and gives you the wisdom you need to act heroically. Standing *up, against,* and *with* requires truth, strength, and compassion, as well as the willingness to conquer your fears.

To develop this 'strength for two', push outside your comfort zone and allow yourself to be stretched and tested – mind, body, and spirit. If it doesn't challenge you, it won't change you. Plus, the more you depend on the strength of God, the more confidence and courage available to you when the moment comes.

Strong Girls, be ready to stand and rise to the occasion in God's strength as He leads you. You are made to be virtuous, wise, and brave! You are made to shine! Be heroic.

THINGS I WOULD TELL MY YOUNGER SELF

"God's presence and power always go with you. Get outside your comfort zone and break free from what other people might think. Get ready to make a difference!"

SEE IT — STOP IT — START IT

1   How can you be spiritually, emotionally, and physically strong enough to help and refresh others?

2.   In what areas do you need to get stronger so you are ready?

3.   Ask God to reveal people in your life who may need a helping hand.

What do you **SEE?** _____

_____

What are you going to **STOP?** _____

_____

What are you going to **START?** _____

_____

Key Verses: Colossians 1:29, Ephesians 6:13, Micah 6:8

Strong Girls is PERFECT for your inner circle of FRIENDS, small groups, YOUTH GROUPS, teams, familes and SCHOOLS.

Strong Girls
IN ACTION

STRONG GIRLS IS FOR EVERY GIRL

The book encourages you to work through each chapter by yourself and then actively engage with others. When you have one-on-one or small group discussions, you share life experiences, challenges, and wisdom, and each of you finds unique ways to apply the truth to your lives.

Engage with your...

- Friends
- Sisters
- Classmates

- Teammates
- Roommates
- Parents

It's perfect for your inner circle of friends, small groups, youth groups, accountability groups, teams, families, and schools.

Plus, you can put this book into action! It's the perfect tool for one-on-one and small groups study and discipleship.

Giving your own hand-written post-it notes to others you want to encourage is the best way to share the truth of God's Word and encourage other girls to be their best.

***Strong Girls* notes have been posted on...**

- mirrors
- laptops
- lockers
- car dashboards
- cell phones
- coffee mug

- whiteboards
- notebooks
- textbooks
- gym bags
- backpacks
- and more...

The most important thing is that you use the power of the *Strong Girls* post-it to help your friends, teammates, sisters – you name it – grow in their faith.

WHERE WILL YOU PUT YOUR POST-ITS?

SHARE THE STRENGTH

Now that you've experienced the power of
Strong Girls yourself, it's time to share it with others.

BUY BOOKS FOR YOUR EVENT OR GROUP
If you'd like to buy bulk copies of *Strong Girls* for your event, conference,
youth group, church, small group, team, or class

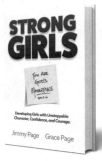

Quantities	Price per book (plus S & H)
5 - 9 Books	$17.95
10 - 49 Books	$16.95
50 - 99 Books	$15.95
100 - 249 Books	$13.95
250+ Books	$11.95

To place your order contact:

Email: orderbooks@BeAStrongGirl.com
Web: BeAStrongGirl.com

BOOK GRACE AND JIMMY TO SPEAK AT YOUR NEXT EVENT
Email: speak@BeAStrongGirl.com

FREE RESOURCES
Make sure you go to the *Strong Girls* website at **BeAStrongGirl.com** to
get free resources and connect with other *Strong Girls*.

The free resources will help you discover what others have learned on
their journey, find new ideas for more strength training devotions, and
find out about upcoming events!

STRONG GIRLS ARE:

KIND HUMBLE GENEROUS
PRETTY JOYFUL **RADIANT**
HONEST FUN PASSIONATE CARING
CAPABLE GRITTY RISK-TAKERS
BRAVE FORGIVEN **BOLD**
FEMININE **CONFIDENT** WISE
FIT ATHLETIC **GRACEFUL** RESILIENT
HOPEFUL **OPTIMISTIC**
GENTLE TALENTED GROWING
VIRTUOUS STRONG
COMPASSIONATE **CREATIVE**
GRATEFUL **POSITIVE** FUNNY
ENCOURAGING DETERMINED
LOVING POWERFUL SENSITIVE
COURAGEOUS
NURTURING SMART
PATIENT FREE
THOUGHTFUL

ABOUT THE AUTHORS

GRACE PAGE is an author, speaker, and disciple-maker. She's a former lacrosse player and current lacrosse coach, FCA huddle leader, church youth leader, and Senior at Liberty University. Grace's mission is to inspire young ladies to love Jesus and live with character, confidence, and courage. Visit her at BeAStrongGirl.com and @BeAStrongGirl37.

JIMMY PAGE has co-authored ten best-selling books including *One Word, One Word for Kids, Daily Wisdom for Men, True Competitor, WisdomWalks, Called to Greatness*, and more. He's a health and wellness expert, freedom warrior, Spartan athlete, podcaster, and former 17-year executive with the Fellowship of Christian Athletes. He's an in-demand speaker on leadership, culture, and human performance for conferences, schools, sports teams, churches, and businesses including the NFL, NCAA, YMCA, NASCAR, Intel, Salvation Army, City of Refuge, Hendrick Motorsports, and many more.

Jimmy is a husband and proud father of four grown kids (including Grace) and resides in Fort Collins, Colorado. He and his wife started a cancer foundation called *Believe Big* following her victory over cancer. His mission is to inspire you to live the unstoppable life.

Visit him at beunstoppable.live or email him at Jimmy@beunstoppable.live.

BOOK A SPEAKER

Want more from the
Strong Girls experience?

Grace and Jimmy travel the country and speak at
conferences, events, churches, colleges, camps, retreats,
ministries, and schools sharing the Strong Girls message.

They do keynotes, workshops, and panel discussions
and will be a perfect addition for your group!

Grace and Jimmy openly and authentically
share their journey as Dad and Daughter
and reveal insights you can only get in person.

If you're looking to spark a movement of
Strong Girls in your community, book them now!

Email speak@BeAStrongGirl.com today!

ACKNOWLEDGEMENTS

This Strong Girls project was truly a 6-year journey. We are incredibly grateful to share this story with millions around the world.

We wanted to give special thanks to:

- Our Heavenly Father who has poured out His unconditional love, grace, and freedom in our lives and has rescued us by grace through faith in His Son Jesus.

- The amazing grace of Jesus who never gives up on us.

- The power of the Holy Spirit who works in us to remind us of the truth, overcome the enemy, and become fully alive in Christ.

- Frank Lugenbeel, the most talented and creative design-man in the world!

- Grace would like to thank her Mom & Dad for their patience, perseverance, and never-ending belief in her. She is also grateful for a few faithful friends who kept pointing her to Jesus – Jaycie, Breezy, Ryan, and Gabi. This would not have been possible without them.

- Jimmy would like to thank his wife Ivelisse for never giving up and for fighting in the spiritual realm with prayer. He is also grateful for the counsel from his watchman and mentor, Dan Webster, who was available 24/7 to give invaluable parenting wisdom and insight.

Made in the USA
Columbia, SC
26 December 2024

50646295R00098